KECHIKA CHRONICLER

Caitlin Press Inc.
3375 Ponderosa Way
Qualicum Beach, BC V9K 2J8
www.caitlinpress.com

Text design by Vici Johnstone
Cover design by Sarah Corsie
Edited by Catherine Edwards
Cover Photo: Willard Freer on the 1934 Bedaux Expedition. Charles Bedaux hired well-known film maker, Floyd Crosby, for the expedition. Crosby also took photographs, including a portrait photograph of each of the members. PA-171477, Library and Archives Canada

Printed in Canada

Caitlin Press Inc. acknowledges financial support from the Government of Canada and the Canada Council for the Arts, and the Province of British Columbia through the British Columbia Arts Council and the Book Publisher's Tax Credit.

Library and Archives Canada Cataloguing in Publication
Kechika chronicler : Willard Freer's Northern BC and Yukon diaries, 1942-1978 / Jay Sherwood.
Sherwood, Jay, 1947-2022, author.

Includes bibliographical references and index.
Canadiana 20220217300 | ISBN 9781773860909 (softcover)
LCSH: Freer, Willard, 1910-—Diaries. | LCSH: Frontier and pioneer life—British Columbia,
   Northern. | LCSH: Frontier and pioneer life—Yukon. | LCGFT: Diaries.
LCC FC3845.N67 S52 2022 | DDC 971.1/8—dc23

# KECHIKA CHRONICLER

Willard Freer's Northern BC and Yukon Diaries, 1942–1975

## JAY SHERWOOD

CAITLIN PRESS 2023

Dedicated to the people who populate Freer's diaries.

# Contents

# Maps

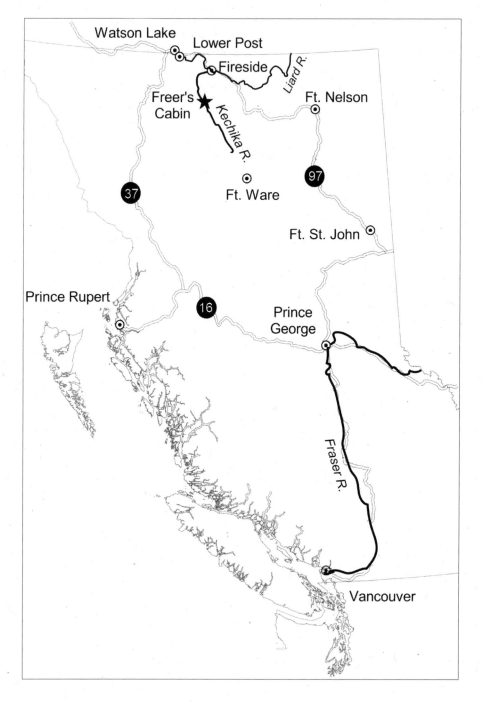

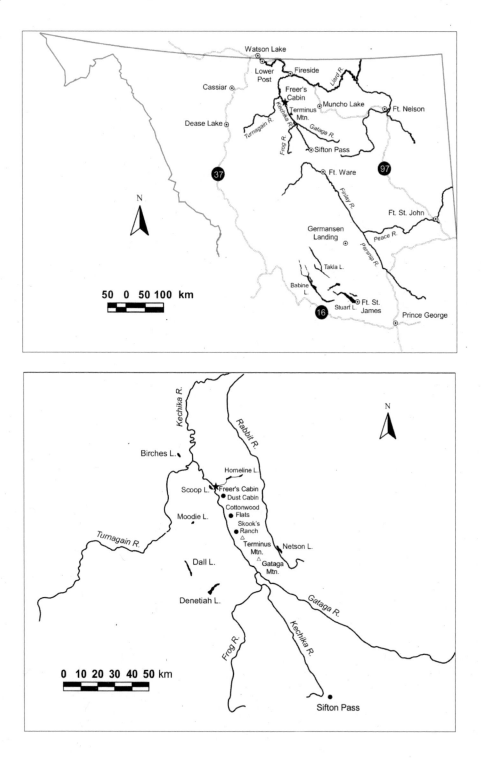

# PREFACE

*Kechika Chronicler* is part of a collaborative project that involves Northern BC Archives, Hudson's Hope Museum, and the families of Willard Freer and Skook Davidson.

Located in the most northerly section of the Rocky Mountain Trench, the Kechika River valley is considered to be one of the most intact watersheds in British Columbia, and one of the most remote. The Kechika has been a homeland and transportation route for Indigenous people for millennia.

In 1939, Skook Davidson first came to the Kechika while packing for the BC government's preliminary survey for a proposed highway from Prince George through the Rocky Mountain Trench to Alaska. Since the survey was going to continue in 1940, the government paid Skook to winter the horses in the Kechika River valley. Skook used the income and opportunity to establish his Diamond J Ranch (named for the diamond hitch used in packing, and John, Skook's first name). At that time, the BC government considered any land not set aside as a reserve for Indigenous people to belong to the Crown.

Three years later, Willard Freer joined Skook at the Diamond J Ranch. Freer worked with Skook until 1949, when he established his own place on a section of land farther north in the Kechika River valley.

Freer's diaries begin in 1942 and continue until 1975. His 1950–51 notebook is the only one that is missing. In Freer's brief but meticulous daily entries, he described his activities and any people that he met. When he was packing, he recorded the amount of time he travelled each day and the location of his campsite. His diaries record his interactions with over a hundred Indigenous people, most of them inhabitants of the Kechika and nearby area. The people who lived closest to him are mentioned many times.

Freer's diaries are the basis for *Kechika Chronicler*, and my thanks goes to his family for lending them for this book. Because there are so many people, places and events recorded in Freer's diaries, a transcription has been made, making it easier for people to search through the contents of the diaries. This transcription will be publicly accessible through the Northern BC Archives website, and the Hudson's Hope Museum.

*Kechika Chronicler* provides an overview of the people that Freer met and his activities. The book includes several sidebars that provide research and background information. They give context to some of the most significant projects and people that Freer describes in his diaries. Willard's diaries are probably the best written records describing life in the Kechika River valley and surrounding area during the mid-twentieth century. This previously unpublished material has many applications to northern BC history and provides readers with an opportunity to learn about Freer's activities and interactions in more detail.

It is fortuitous that *Kechika Chronicler* is being published at this time, for in the past year a box of Skook Davidson material has been donated to the Northern BC Archives by his great-nephew, Gord Yule. It is currently being processed. In addition, a seventeen-minute film of Freer driving a riverboat on the Kechika and Turnagain Rivers in 1977 has become publicly available. All of this material will provide new information and perspective for people who are interested in the history of northern BC.

# INTRODUCTION

*Kechika Chronicler* is the story of Willard Freer (1910–1981) and his experiences in northern BC and Yukon, told mainly through more than thirty years' worth of personal diaries. Freer lived in the remote Kechika River valley where he had a cabin and trapline and interacted with the Indigenous people who inhabited the area. As a packer he was involved in many important projects that took place throughout northern BC and southern Yukon. Willard also worked at a couple of lodges on the Alaska Highway, and he describes life along this important road. Freer's diaries are the best written record of the Indigenous people who lived in the Kechika River valley in the mid-twentieth century. They also contain information and details about many prominent people and events in the area where he lived and worked.

Willard was born in Kamloops, British Columbia, on April 19, 1910, a few months after his parents had emigrated from the United States. Freer's ancestors had been farmers for many generations. The earliest documentation of the Freer family in North America is a ship record of Hugo Freer arriving in the city of New York in July 1675. The Freers were farmers in New York state for several generations. In the early 1830s, Jonas Elisha Freer moved to Michigan, which was still a territory, to farm. His grandson, Jonas Melville Freer, born in Michigan in 1855, continued westward to Dakota Territory in the early 1880s where his son, George Elisha Freer, was born in 1885. In early 1910, George and Edith Key left North Dakota to search for agricultural land in Canada, abetted by the fact that Edith was pregnant. On February 11, George and Edith were married in Miles City, Montana. Three days later, they entered Canada at the Coutts/Sweetgrass border crossing. They journeyed north to the Canadian Pacific Railway line and travelled by train to Kamloops where their first child, Willard Melvin, was born on April 19.

When Willard was three weeks old, his parents drove by wagon to Fort George (present day Prince George). In the 1911 census, George Freer was recorded as a rancher living on rented land near Cluculz Lake. This lake in the Central Interior region of British Columbia was near the Grand Trunk Pacific Railway, which was being constructed across northern BC at that time. By fall of that year, Freer had filed for a pre-emption along the Chilako River southwest of Fort George, and a second son, Merle, was born there in October. In addition to the farm, George probably worked on construction

The Freer family at their farm on Bear Flat (Freer on far right) shortly before he moved to Hudson's Hope. Willard Freer Family collection

of the Grand Trunk Pacific Railway. A daughter, Ella, was born a year later, and in the fall of 1913, Freer received a Crown grant to the land along the Chilako River.

However, George and Edith believed that the land was "not open enough and the soil burned out," and they decided to go north to the Peace River district. Edith was pregnant again, so the family temporarily split. Edith took the three children and went back to her parents' home in Missouri where the fourth child, Harold, was born on June 19, 1914. Meanwhile, George and a companion spent the late fall and winter of 1913 and 1914 trapping in the Crooked River area north of Prince George. In early spring, the two men travelled down the Crooked and Parsnip Rivers to the Peace, then proceeded down this river valley to Hudson's Hope, where they sold their furs.

George continued down the Peace River valley toward the Hudson's Bay Company (HBC) post at Fort St. John. Along the way he found land that he thought would be productive at a place called Bear Flat, which was located on the north side of the Peace River adjacent to Cache Creek. During the summer of 1914, he earned money cutting wood for the *D.A. Thomas*, a steamboat that plied the Peace River.

In the fall, George was reunited with his family. They spent the winter in northern Alberta, and George filed for his pre-emption at the land office in Grouard. At that time, governments did not consult with Indigenous peoples regarding their connection to their traditional territories.

The Freers purchased supplies and livestock and, in late winter and early spring 1915, travelled to their homestead along the Peace. Willard wrote about the last section of the trip, from Fort St. John. "My next brother and I were put on a pack horse in two boxes and rode that way for 22 miles [35 kilometres] where the parents settled down."

Willard grew up at Bear Flat. Of the seven Freer children, he was the one most influenced by the remote wilderness to the north and west. When he was about twenty, he moved to Hudson's Hope, a small community farther upstream on the Peace River that was closer to the Rocky Mountain wilderness. Around 1936, Willard moved northwest, taking up a trapline in the Ingenika River valley. (The Ingenika flows into the Finlay River, one of the headwater rivers of the Peace.) In 1942, Willard ventured north into the remote Kechika River valley, which is less than a hundred kilometres from the Yukon boundary. He worked and lived at the ranch of the famous packer Skook Davidson for several years before building his own cabin farther north along the Kechika. There Willard lived for the rest of his life, with some intervals spent working at the Fireside Inn on the Alaska Highway (near the junction of the Kechika and Liard Rivers).

Willard was at home in this remote area: self-reliant, confident in his ability to live in the wilderness and comfortable with his surroundings. Almost everyone who knew Willard described the same character traits. He was quiet and shy. As a worker, he was reliable. Willard, like many people who lived in remote areas, was also very versatile. Among his many abilities, he could pack horses, operate a motor boat, trap animals for fur, and cook, along with building and repairing items. When he worked at the Fireside Inn on the Alaska Highway, he did a variety of jobs: operating the gas pump, repairing tires, basic carpentry, cooking and shovelling snow.

Although Willard was quiet around people, he had an important way of communicating. In a letter that he wrote in 1935, he stated that he had started keeping a diary when he left home. Unfortunately, his early diaries have been lost. In the summer of 1939, while Freer was away working, the BC Provincial Police investigated his neighbour Frank "Shorty" Weber as a suspect in a local murder. The police seized Freer's diaries from his trapping cabin as potential evidence. Freer wrote to the police requesting the return of his diaries, but he never received them. Fortunately, Freer had made copies of his diaries for the summers of 1932 and 1934. His diary for 1934 is particularly important because he was a member of the Bedaux Expedition.

Freer's existing diaries begin in the spring of 1942, when he was still living in the Ingenika River valley, and continue until 1975. The notebook for 1950 and 1951 is missing, and the January to September 1961 section has been removed. The diaries from 1942 to 1972 are in the possession of the Freer family, while the 1973 to 1975 notebook is housed at the Alaska Highway Museum in Fort Nelson. Freer presumably kept a diary beyond that time, but there is no record of its existence.

Throughout his adult life, Freer wrote a daily journal. The entries are usually brief and direct, with minimal philosophizing. They are often repetitive, describing daily routines. However, the cumulative narrative of Freer's diaries provides a rare look into the history of one of British Columbia's most remote areas.

The pantheon of people recorded in Freer's diaries include many notable individuals who lived and worked in the Kechika River valley and along the Alaska Highway. Willard's journals provide details about specific events in the lives of these people. There are many references to the famous bush pilots Stan Bridcut and George Dalziel. He notes several prospectors who are well-known in northern BC and the Yukon.

Willard's work involved extensive travel though northern BC and Yukon. His diaries provide details about the locations he visited. In particular, Freer kept an important record of travel on the Davie Trail between Fort Ware and Lower Post. For every overnight trip he made, Freer recorded the campsite he used, and the amount of time he spent travelling each day.

During the 1940s and 1950s, the Kaska and Kwadacha Tsek'ene still followed their traditional yearly rounds in the Kechika drainage. Freer's diaries detail the lives and routines of numerous Indigenous people over many years. Some of them are mentioned over a hundred times in Freer's diaries. By all accounts, Willard had good relationships with the Indigenous people. In the remote northern BC and Yukon region, where there were few people, working co-operatively was important.

Willard lived and worked at Skook Davidson's Diamond J Ranch during most of the 1940s and at intervals in the 1950s, so his journals provide considerable information about Skook and life at the ranch. In addition, there are recently located fragments of Skook's personal diaries from the 1940s and 1950s. These records show the impact that Skook and Willard had on the ecology of the Kechika valley through their sizeable herd of horses and the economic effect on the Indigenous people through the establishment of an informal trade store during the trapping season where goods and fur were exchanged.

Freer's diaries contain considerable information about daily life in the lodges along the Alaska Highway. There are numerous entries describing the activities of both Jack and Flo Christy, who operated the lodge at Lower Post, and Margo and Ken Windrem, owners of the Fireside Inn for many years. At Fireside, Freer had a close friendship with the Nelms family, particularly George, who was the head of Highway Department maintenance for that section of the Alaska Highway, and the Nelms family is frequently mentioned in diary entries in the 1960s and early 1970s.

Freer was involved in many important projects in northern BC and Yukon. He was a member of the famous 1934 Bedaux Expedition. Freer was a packer for BC and federal government survey crews for several summers; worked on the British Columbia-Yukon Boundary Survey for four years; was employed on Geological Survey of Canada (GSC) crews for several years; and spent three field seasons on the BC government's Forest Inventory program. Willard also packed for a couple of large mining exploration companies and was a hunting guide for Robin Dalziel and other guide outfitters.

Freer's diaries can also be used to monitor events like the weather and snowfall. In the winter, when he lived at Skook's ranch or at his cabin, he recorded the temperature in the morning, at midday, and in the evening. He also noted snowfalls. Willard recorded the date that the Kechika froze over in the fall, and when the ice melted off the river in the spring. He also noted his first observations of birds in the spring.

Freer's journals reflect some of the prejudices common in that time. Willard drank liquor, but usually in moderation. In his diaries, he wrote disapprovingly about instances where people drank excessively to the extent that it impaired their judgment, behaviour and ability to work. Many of Freer's interactions were with Indigenous people, so some of his diary entries appear to depict the stereotype of their relationship to alcohol. However, he equally decried Skook's famous drinking binges at Lower Post and the behaviour of other workers at Skook's ranch who started drinking almost immediately after arriving at that community.

Similarly, Freer thought that a person should work hard when there was labour that needed to be done. In his diary, he sometimes mentions a person whom he felt was not doing their share of the work. Although this can appear to be a stereotype when applied to Indigenous people, Freer's disapproval was more generally of laziness.

In his diaries, it appears that Willard used the name(s) of the Indigenous person(s) if he was writing about an individual or small group of people that he knew. If it was a larger group of people, or individuals that he didn't know, Willard used Indian(s), the term generally used at that time to describe Indigenous Peoples.

There is one stereotype that appears frequently in Freer's journals. Freer, Skook Davidson, and many other people in the area viewed the wolf as a predator to be eradicated. The BC government had a bounty on wolves and supplied poison to be used in an effort to kill them. Skook brought a herd of horses into the Kechika valley in the fall of 1939, and thereby changed the ecology of the area. For Skook and Freer (when he had his own herd), one of the important and ongoing duties of maintaining horses was protecting them from wolves. This meant watching for signs of wolves, shooting them if possible, and poisoning them if they stayed close to their dwellings. In the winter, Freer often went out to check on the horses and make sure that they stayed in bunches large enough to provide security. He would also move the horses to different locations to ensure that they found enough feed to survive the long winter. To Freer and Skook, the stereotype of wolves was part of a personal struggle to maintain their livelihood in the Kechika River valley.

The diaries of Willard Freer, which chronicle over thirty years of life in northern BC, are a unique account, providing a gateway to many of the people who lived there and some of the important events that occurred.

# The Land and the People

The Rocky Mountain Trench is a major geographical feature in British Columbia. It is a broad valley three to sixteen kilometres wide located between the western slope of the Rocky Mountains and the eastern slope of mountain ranges like the Columbia, Omineca and Cassiar. The trench, which begins in northern Montana, runs in a northwest/southeast direction for over 1,500 kilometres through British Columbia, almost to the border with Yukon. Several of British Columbia's major rivers flow through sections of the trench, and the divides between the rivers are at low elevation.

The Kechika River is the most northerly river in the Rocky Mountain Trench. From Sifton Pass, it flows north for about 230 kilometres to the Liard River. About one third of the way down the river, the Rocky Mountains end at Terminus Mountain. North of this location, the trench begins to become more indistinct, ending approximately at the Liard River. Much of the land is boreal forest, and there is a large population of big game mammals. Renowned wildlife conservation scientist Dr. John Weaver states: "The 300-kilometre stretch of Rocky Mountain Trench (which is so prominent it can be seen from space) that bisects the Muskwa-Kechika is the last wild section of this amazing geologic feature left in B.C." (Weaver describes this in more detail in a July 2019 Wildlife Conservation Society Canada Conservation Report.)

The Cassiar Mountains on the west side of the Rocky Mountain Trench create a rain shadow for the Kechika River valley. At the time Freer lived there, the depth of snowfall in the winter was usually less than forty centimetres. The temperature normally went down to −40°C for several days in the winter, but the cold spells seldom lasted longer than a few days before a warm wind from the south blew up through the trench.

Currently, the Kechika River valley is considered one of the most intact watersheds in British Columbia and is a key part of the Muskwa-Kechika Management Area. The Muskwa-Kechika Management Area Act states that its intent is to

> maintain in perpetuity the wilderness quality, and the diversity and abundance of wildlife and the ecosystems on which it depends, while allowing resource development and use in parts of the M-KMA designated for those purposes,

The Kechika River flowing through the broad Rocky Mountain Trench. Image I-64838 courtesy the Royal BC Museum and Archives

including recreation, hunting, trapping, timber harvesting, mineral exploration and mining, and oil and gas exploration and development.

The management area is largely comprised of the Kechika River drainage on the west side of the Rocky Mountains, and the Muskwa on the east. Weaver states that:

The Muskwa-Kechika is one of the most intact wild areas remaining on the planet. Four times the size of Vancouver Island, it is an area with few roads (98 per cent roadless) and little resource development. The result is intact forests, clean water, and healthy wildlife populations.

Weaver describes what makes the Muskwa-Kechika area unique.

It… has a high level of habitat diversity due to its varied topography, different landforms, and many lakes and wetlands—all of which provide options for plants and animals to adapt as climate heating accelerates. In particular, this diversity offers wildlife important "climate ramps"—the

48 Mile Meadow on trail to Lower Post. This was one of the most frequently used campsites on the Davie trail. It was located about 30 km west of the Kechika River crossing at Mile 66, a day's travel by horse. Skook Davidson Family collection

ability to move to higher elevations along slopes leading up to the Continental Divide or along river valleys from mouth to headwaters.

Because the entire Kechika watershed is virtually intact from its source to its mouth, and from valley floor to peak, scientists contend that it will be a refugia as climate change occurs, because wildlife and plants will be able to find their niche among the valley's ecosystems.

The Rocky Mountain Trench has been an important transportation corridor for Indigenous people and also forms part of the ancestral lands of many First Nations. Two First Nations, the Tsek'ene and the Kaska Dena, inhabited the Kechika valley when Willard Freer came to the area in 1942. The Tsek'ene live mainly along the upper Finlay River. In the 1920s, free traders established a post called Whitewater or Fort Ware at a location near the junction of the Finlay and Kwadacha Rivers. The Kwadacha band of the Tsek'ene live in this area. In the 1940s, the area around Sifton Pass was the traditional territory of Mac McCook and his descendants, who are part of the Kwadacha band. Their territory extends into the upper Kechika drainage, down to the Gataga River, the major tributary on the east side of the Kechika.

Amos Alec (centre in white shirt) and his family in the early 1980s at their trapping cabin at Bag Lake. Willard had frequent contact with the Alec family for many years. Amos had his own guide outfitting area along the Turnagain River for a few years. It was in the vicinity of his winter trapline. Chris Widrig states that Amos was a great guy and respected Kaska elder. Photo courtesy of Chris Widrig

The second First Nation inhabiting the Kechika River valley, the Kaska Dena, live in the southern part of Yukon and Northwest Territories and northwestern BC. The Kechika valley north of the Gataga is considered the southern limit of traditional Kaska territory. It also includes land along the western tributaries of the Kechika, like the Frog and Turnagain Rivers.

At and near Lower Post, there is a third Indigenous group living in the area: the Tahltan, whose home territory is centred around Telegraph Creek on the Stikine River. There is a traditional trade route from the Pacific Ocean up the Stikine through Tahltan territory to Telegraph Creek. From there the route went overland to the north, crossing over a divide to the head of Dease Lake. It went down the lake to the Dease River, and down that river to the Liard. In the nineteenth century, the Hudson's Bay Company used this trade route as the easiest way to access its posts in the upper Liard basin. Trading posts were established at Telegraph Creek, Dease Lake, McDame along the Dease River, and Lower Post along the Liard River. Some of the Tahltan followed this trade route and moved to the Lower Post

Mrs. Amos Alec. Honigmann was a well-known sociologist who spent many years studying the Kaska culture. When he was at Lower Post in 1945, Honigmann took several excellent photographs of the Indigenous residents. This is one of the few pictures that has identification. Photo courtesy Dr. Bryan Cummins; photo permission John Honigmann family

area. Most of them were involved in the trading business. In her master's thesis in sociology on the community of Lower Post in the early 1970s, Joyce Nelms estimated that about a quarter of the community's population was Tahltan.

There is a traditional trail (usually called the Davie Trail) between Fort Ware and Lower Post on the Liard River. From Fort Ware, it follows the Rocky Mountain Trench northwest over Sifton Pass and down the east side of the Kechika River. On the upper Kechika, the trail crosses the Gataga, a sizeable river and the northern boundary of Tsek'ene territory. From the Gataga, it is about thirty-five kilometres to the Diamond J Ranch, which is located on the north side of Matulka Creek at the base of Terminus Mountain. Continuing north down the Kechika River valley about fifteen kilometres, there is a large area of level land called Cottonwood Flats that extends for over ten kilometres down the Kechika and is three to five kilometres wide. Some of Skook Davidson's horses would often be seen in the flats, and there was a small, dirt floor cabin for shelter. Approximately ten kilometres farther north along the Davie Trail, there was Dust Cabin, which also provided basic shelter and was about a day's travel from the Diamond J.

A few kilometres north of Dust Cabin, the Davie Trail crossed Horneline Creek. Here, a side trail went east for about twenty kilometres over a mountain pass to Horneline Lake. (Although Horneline Creek and Horneline Lake are the official geographical names, both are referred to as Horn in

Freer's diary entries.) From 1940 to 1951, this drainage and the Rabbit River to the east was part of the government-registered trapline of Fred Forsberg. His wife was Annie McCook, a member of the Tsek'ene from Kwadacha, and the Rabbit River drainage was probably part of their traditional territory. In 1951, Willard Freer acquired this trapline.

Almost directly west from Horneline Creek, on the west side of the Kechika, is Scoop Lake. Bush pilots often use this lake for delivering supplies and people to this section of the Kechika. When Frank Cooke Jr. purchased the western half of Skook's guiding territory, Scoop Lake became his base, and he built several structures there. Farther north, the Turnagain River, the largest tributary of the Kechika, enters from the west. Below the Turnagain, the Davie Trail crosses the wide Kechika River. It proceeds northwest through the Liard plateau toward the Hudson's Bay Company post and the community of Lower Post, located on the north bank of the Liard River near the junction with the Dease River. At this location, there is the largest river crossing on the trail. Sometimes people go upstream, cross the Dease River and then cross the Liard. There is also a location called McNab Point near Lower Post that people sometimes use.

During the nineteenth century, the main contact between the Indigenous people and the newcomers was through the Hudson's Bay Company fur trade. In the 1870s, there was a gold rush into the Cassiar region, and a trading post called Chee House was established at the junction of the Kechika and Turnagain Rivers. At the end of the nineteenth century, during the Klondike Gold Rush, the Kechika River valley became part of an all-Canadian route to Yukon. Inspector J.D. Moodie of the Northwest Mounted Police was given the responsibility for establishing a trail that could be used to reach the Klondike goldfields. Moodie Creek and Moodie Lakes in the Kechika drainage are named for him. (The Fort Nelson Heritage Museum has a cattle skull that Freer found in the Kechika valley, an indication that one of the Klondike cattle herds travelled along this route.)

In 1930, a road was constructed from Prince George to Summit Lake, the headwaters of the Crooked River. From Prince George, supplies were driven to this location and loaded onto motorized river freight boats that could each carry several tonnes of supplies. The goods were transported down the Crooked River to the Parsnip, down this river to Finlay Forks, and up the Finlay to Fort Grahame and Fort Ware. This made it easier and cheaper to access supplies in the Finlay River area. During the 1930s, the riverboats were busy from late spring to early fall hauling supplies to Fort Grahame and Fort Ware. There was mining activity in the area, trapping in the winter and other economic ventures. Float planes took off and landed on the Finlay River. Fort Ware became the economic centre for the inhabitants of a large part of the Kechika River valley.

However, in 1942, construction of the Alaska Highway began, and the route passed through Lower Post but not Fort Ware. By the late 1940s, the economic centre for most of the Kechika River valley inhabitants had switched to the Alaska Highway. Initially it was to Lower Post, but by the 1950s, Watson Lake in Yukon territory became the commercial centre of the region. The community has a large airfield that was constructed during World War II. (Watson Lake Air Terminal Building, built in 1942, is the only air terminal building from the Northwest Staging Route that's still in use in Yukon. In 2019, it was declared a Yukon historical site.) Supplies and food could arrive either from the Alaska Highway or by air. Almost every air flight that Freer took to the Kechika valley originated at Watson Lake.

When Willard Freer came to the Kechika valley in 1942, the Indigenous inhabitants still maintained a largely traditional life, living in small family groups and following the seasonal events through their territory. The area had an abundant fur-bearing population, so trapping provided income that was used to purchase supplies. But World War II and the Alaska Highway would bring major changes to the way of life of the inhabitants of the Kechika valley.

# Before Coming to the Kechika:
## 1915–1942

During 1915, George and Edith Freer began developing the farm at Bear Flat. Edith described their initial housing: "We lived in a tent 12'x 14' [3.6 by 4.2 metres] and a sleep-tent on one side. We lived in these tents the first summer and winter of 1915–16, with nothing for heat except a cook stove and Hudson's Bay blankets. During the winter a tarp was put over the tent roof to keep the snow off. It was very comfortable all winter." The first summer was spent clearing and breaking land and haying. A log cabin was constructed during the summer of 1916.

The farm became productive for the Freer family. They grew crops, including wheat; raised cattle and other livestock; and had a large garden. The surrounding countryside provided game, fish and berries. Trapping and freighting for the Hudson's Bay Company also brought in income. A few other settlers came to Bear Flat and, by the early 1920s, there were enough children for a one-room school. Edith became postmistress for the community in 1924 (the appointment was actually in George's name).

The Freer family continued to grow and, by the early 1920s, eight children had been born, with one dying in infancy. Five of the surviving children were boys, and as they got older, they helped on the farm. Around 1923, George Freer expanded the farm by purchasing an adjacent quarter section (sixty-five hectares) from the Robinson family. The property included a newly built, larger house that could better accommodate the growing children.

George probably hoped that Willard, the eldest son, would become a farmer also. Initially, it appeared that he would. In both 1929 and 1930, Willard filed for homestead land, but he did not follow through with either of his applications. Instead, around 1930, he moved to Hudson's Hope up the Peace River. It was a larger community than Bear Flat, but it was closer to the mountains and the largely wilderness area to the north and west.

In a letter dated December 25, 1935, Freer wrote: "I left home 5 years ago and have kept a diary every day since." When Freer arrived at Hudson's Hope, the Depression had already started, and Freer had to take whatever work he could find. He must have been determined to live independently, for he did not return to the farm at Bear Flat. Unfortunately, his diaries from his years at Hudson's Hope no longer exist, except for a segment in 1932, and more importantly, his record of his adventures on the 1934 Bedaux Expedition.

## 1932

Freer's 1932 diary segment began on March 24 when he was working at the Gething sawmill. The book *Hudson's Hope and Her Pioneers* describes the sawmill and Freer's diaries.

> There were factors which made life easier for the settlers. Wes Gething established the sawmill on Beryl Prairie and settlers were able to bring in their own logs to be sawn into the lumber they need[ed] and to work extra time to pay for the sawing or they could pay with extra saw logs. A diary of Willard Freer's written over a period of time at the mill mentions men coming and going all the time. One would wonder at the very rapid turnover of personnel. It merely depicted the various fellows getting the lumber they needed and working to pay their bills.

Local historian Martin Kyllo wrote: "In early 1931 the Gethings moved their sawmill to Beryl Prairie and bought the steam engine from the old Peace River Gold Dredging sawmill to power it. Work was created for several of the local people and lumber sawn for construction of buildings on Beryl Prairie and in Hudson's Hope." Dave Kyllo noted that a land reserve on the prairie had been lifted in 1929 and several pre-emptions were made there.

Undoubtedly, the highlight of the summer for Willard was the boat trip with King (Quentin) Gething, who had a contract to take mail to the people and small communities along the upper Peace and Finlay Rivers. His route went from Hudson's Hope to Fort Grahame, a distance of about 275 kilometres. He made one trip a month (departing from Hudson's Hope on the twelfth day) from May to October when the river was open. During the winter, he travelled up the river in January and March. Freer had an opportunity to go with King and help him. It was his first visit to this remote area.

Freer and King Gething travelled on the portage over Rocky Mountain Canyon on the Peace River and camped there on July 13. The next morning, they loaded King's large boat. In addition to the mail and some supplies, King had several passengers.

On July 15 they stopped at Jim Beattie's household; at W.A. Mahaffey's, where King borrowed a tent; and at Carbon River Jones's place, where they stayed overnight. They had a group of passengers including Lillian and Vesta Gething, Mrs. F.C. Gaylor and her two children, and also Mrs. Ruxton and Mrs. Vaihes. "The women are out for a week's holiday," Freer wrote.

Each day, as Gething proceeded up the Peace River, there were several stops to pick up and drop off mail, passengers and supplies. There were no difficulties going through the Ne-parle-pas Rapids, and by July 17, Gething and his entourage had reached Finlay Forks. The next day they travelled up the Finlay River, and in the evening of July 19, they arrived at the Hudson's Bay Company post of Fort Grahame.

In his diary entry for July 20, Freer wrote: "This is my first trip to Fort Grahame. We stayed here up until noon and then pulled for the homeward trip. This is the end of the mail route." During the return trip, Freer wrote: "We stopped at all the camps that we came to, to pick up mail or throw off something." At Carbon River Jones's homestead, they picked up the group of women they had met on their trip upstream. Freer and the passengers went over the portage and back to Hudson's Hope on July 23. The trip was an exciting adventure for Freer and likely whetted his appetite to spend more time in this remote region. He would return within a few years.

In August 1932, a visitor arrived at Hudson's Hope. His hunting expedition in the area led to an event that had an impact on the history of northern BC, and on Willard Freer's personal life. Charles Bedaux was born in France in 1886 and immigrated to the United States in 1906. In 1917 he started his own scientific management company, and within a few years, became one of the leaders in this field. In 1920 Bedaux moved to the city of New York, where his company expanded rapidly. Within a few years, he established branch offices in several countries around the world, including Canada, and became one of the wealthiest people in the United States.

Bedaux went on expensive hunting trips, often to places outside the United States. He also became interested in investing in gold-mining operations. In 1926, with his wife, son, and a group of friends, Bedaux came to the Cassiar Ranch northwest of Fort St. James. The owner, Bob McCorkell, was an American who had moved to British Columbia and was developing gold mines in the remote Omineca district to the north and west. He and his brother Bert had horses at the ranch that they used to transport supplies to their mines and bring back the gold. They also used the horses to take people on hunting trips. From the Cassiar Ranch, the McCorkells took Bedaux and his group on a hunting trip to the Thutade Lake area that lasted about a month.

In 1932, Bedaux wanted to take another hunting trip to British Columbia, this time to the Peace River district. With his wife and a small group of friends, he came to Edmonton, where they hired Jack Bocock to organize an expedition. Bocock had an MA in geology from the University of British Columbia. In 1929 and 1930, as a member of the provincial government's PGE Resources Survey, Bocock had evaluated the mineral resources in the Peace River district. Earlier in the summer of 1932, he had worked on a mining venture in the upper Peace River. Bedaux's party and Bocock travelled to Hudson's Hope where they hired Bob Beattie, a local packer, who organized a six-week hunting trip into the Rocky Mountains north of Hudson's Hope.

At the end of the trip, the *Peace River Block News* reported: "It is rumoured that Mr. Bedaux intends within the next two years to ship three especially large and specially constructed caterpillar tractors that will blaze a road to Redfern Lake." In 1930 Bedaux made the first automobile trip across Africa, from Mombasa to Casablanca. Now he was beginning to contemplate a similar type of trip across part of northern BC.

## 1933

Bedaux was also interested in investing in a gold-mining operation in the Peace River area and he asked Bocock to find one for him. It was the middle of the Depression, and Bocock was reluctant to have Bedaux spend a large amount of money because of uncertain economic conditions. However, Bedaux persisted, and Bocock arranged for him to invest some money in a small gold-dredging operation on the upper Peace River in which he was a partner.

In the summer of 1933, this mining company needed some employees for their operation. Freer was one of the people that Bocock hired. During 1933, Bedaux continued to develop plans for a motorized expedition across northern BC, and in September, he purchased five half-track vehicles from the French vehicle manufacturer André Citroën. These vehicles had wheels on the front and a caterpillar track on the back. Citroën had constructed similar vehicles for trips across Africa and Europe. In the fall of 1933, Bedaux hired Jack Bocock to organize his expedition.

## 1934—BEDAUX EXPEDITION

The Bedaux Expedition was one of the most unusual events in the history of northern British Columbia. In 1934, Charles Bedaux attempted to drive five half-track Citroën vehicles across northern BC. He spent over $250,000 on this expedition in the middle of the Depression, and his extravagance led the event to be nicknamed the "champagne safari."

Bocock hired two British Columbia land surveyors. Frank Swannell, who had spent many years in the northern part of the province, was selected geographer to map the terrain along the expedition's route. Surveyor Ernest Lamarque was chosen to locate a route across northern BC. Bedaux hired Floyd Crosby, a young Hollywood filmmaker, to take movie footage of the adventure.

Over the winter and spring of 1933 and 1934, Bocock procured supplies and hired a large number of people. Bedaux and the five Citroëns with their passengers were the main feature of the expedition, but they were supported by many men who were packers and cut trail. Bocock hired mostly local people for these positions. On March 23 he wrote to Freer: "I am wondering whether or not you are wanting work for the coming summer? If so, I can offer you a job starting early in May." The pay would be about double the average rate in the district and the work would last until about October 15. Bocock also wrote: "Please do not mention that I have offered you a job because I have had dozens of applications from all over the Peace River country.... I am offering you the job because we must have men of the right type and I was very satisfied with your work last year."

The Bedaux Expedition was divided into four groups. Ernest Lamarque and a small crew had the responsibility for locating a route that the Citroëns could navigate. Tommy Wilde was in charge of a crew that cleared a route for the Citroëns to drive through. Nick Geake's advance freight party had over fifty pack horses and carried the gasoline, food and supplies that would be needed on the expedition. These three groups started from Fort St. John, while Bedaux and the five Citroëns (the main part of the expedition) began in Edmonton and followed dirt roads to Fort St. John.

The Bedaux Expedition was well-chronicled by its participants. Several members of the main group kept diaries. Among the cowboys on the trip, Bob White wrote a detailed memoir titled *Bannock and Beans*, while Cecil Pickell wrote a short account. Freer was the only cowboy who kept a daily diary.

Freer's diary began on June 24 at Hudson's Hope. Freer, along with cowboys Bob White and Bob Godberson, who also resided in Hudson's Hope, built a raft and travelled down the Peace River to Fort St. John to join the expedition.

The next morning, the three men arrived at the old Hudson's Bay Company post along the river, and then walked about seven kilometres to the town of Fort St. John. They met Edward "Nick" Geake, who was in charge of the advance freight party, and set up camp about one and a half kilometres north of town.

The group departed on July 4 at noon, following the main trail that headed northwest toward the Halfway River valley. In addition to the three men from Hudson's Hope and Nick Geake, there was Art McLean from the Fort St. John area and Ernie Peterson, an experienced packer from the North Pine region.

Meanwhile, the main Bedaux Expedition with the five Citroën vehicles departed from Edmonton on July 6, travelling on dirt roads. It had been a wet spring and the roads turned into a thick mud called "gumbo" that made progress slow. It took eleven days to reach Fort St. John, and by the time

Rafting the Peace River to Fort St. John (Freer on left). Bob White Family collection

they departed from there on July 22, the expedition was already a week behind schedule.

Progress became slower and conditions became worse after leaving Fort St. John. Bedaux soon realized that the Citroën half-tracks were ill-equipped for a trek across northern BC. On August 9, the expedition reached the Halfway River where Bedaux decided to abandon the vehicles.

The route continued up the Halfway River valley. In his diary entry for July 15, Freer wrote: "None of us boys are getting along with Geake. He is too much of a slave driver." After this camp, the group left the Halfway River valley and continued travelling north along the east side of the Rocky Mountains. In one of his diary entries, Freer noted that there was "trouble brewing amongst the men" in their relationship with Geake.

The advance freight party reached the Prophet River on July 26. Two days later they met Cecil Pickell and Earl Cushing from the trail-cutting crew. They had come back to pick up more food, and they camped with Geake's group. The men must have talked about the personnel situation because Geake decided to have Cecil Pickell join the advance freight party while Freer went with Tommy Wilde's trail-cutting crew. Freer was pleased. "Oh boy! Am I tickled. Cecil Pickell and I traded jobs. To hell with Geake." Freer and Earl Cushing returned to the work camp with food on August 2.

On August 17, the crew reached Bedaux Pass where they learned important information. Freer wrote: "J.B. Bocock, head of the Bedaux Sub-Arctic

This is one of the five Citroëns that Bedaux purchased for the expedition.
Bob White Family collection

Expedition arrived in camp to everyone's surprise. Jack MacDougall and
Jack Bocock left the tractors at the north fork of the Halfway River on the
7th of August. They came on to stop us cutting tractor road. They are taking
the freight horses back to help the last and main outfit."

After abandoning the vehicles, the Bedaux Expedition lost its main rai-
son d'être, and became another horseback trip across northern BC. The trail
only needed to be cleared enough for horse travel. The trail crew reached
Whitewater on September 11. Freer wrote: "We all repaired our pack outfit.
All of us had to buy a bunch of new clothes." He also noted: "We had our
first fresh vegetables since we left Fort St. John and they were good."

The men then travelled northwest on the Davie Trail. They reached Sifton Pass on September 22 and camped about two kilometres farther north,
where they waited for Bedaux. While there, Freer noted ominously that
three horses had developed hoof rot and had to be shot. Three days later, Bedaux arrived. After discussion among the expedition leaders, Bedaux made
the decision to continue to Dease Lake. However, when three more horses
were found to have hoof rot, Bedaux realized that he was not going to be
able to proceed safely any farther. Freer wrote: "I went and stopped the trail
cutters. This is the end of our trek through the mountains. We are in retreat.
We are losing too many horses."

In his diary, Freer described the situation the next day: "None of us
wanted to retreat, we were all for going ahead, but the boss says retreat and

that is what it is. Edgar Dopp, Bill & Charlie Blackman camped at La-marque's turn off. The rest of us camped in Sifton Pass."

Although the expedition was not going to reach Telegraph Creek, Bedaux was not in a hurry to finish. He wanted to spend some time doing more filming for the movie he hoped Floyd Crosby would make. The expedition stayed at the pass on September 29. In his entry, Freer wrote: "We did not move today. We are working for the movies. We are all movie stars now." The expedition spent the last day of the month in dramatic fashion. Freer wrote: "We did not move. We are working for the movies. We are having forest fires, the camp burning and everybody leaving in a hurry, horses stampeding with the packs and I don't know what. It snowed last night. The wild west pictures!"

The expedition moved back to Fox Lake on October 1, and two horses had to be shot because they had hoof rot. The next day they arrived at Fox Pass, where they stopped to spend another day filming. Freer wrote: "Twenty head of horses were packed for a stampede. The main outfit were all carrying packs and were leaving the country by foot—that was for the movies. The trail cutters weren't in the picture." There was a surprise during the filming: "E.W.C. Lamarque and Jack Stone arrived back. He was thru to Telegraph Creek. They were 11 ½ days back from Telegraph Creek."

The expedition arrived back in Whitewater on October 6. Two days later, Freer was part of a group of twelve men who took the horses down to the Ingenika River to winter. On October 11, the "Bedaux outfit arrived by boat and brought all the outfit across. We stayed…. We swam the horses. Bedaux went on. They will wait at Deserters Canyon." Two days of travel brought the men to Deserters Canyon. At Ben Cork's place, at the foot of the canyon, the men left the horses that they were riding. "We are finished with the horses for this season. We went to Fort Grahame by boat. There are six boats, quite a flotilla," Freer wrote.

On October 16, the cowboys arrived at Hudson's Hope. October 19 was the final day. "We did nothing all day outside of wait for our pay. We took in a big chicken feed at Ferguson's put on by our boss, Mr. Bedaux…. Most of the boys either sang or made speeches for a while after the supper. We went to a dance at the school."

Freer's final entry for the expedition was made on October 20: "Our last payday—too bad. Bedaux and all the men left for their homes in the different districts of BC…. Well, this is the end of the Bedaux Sub-Arctic Expedition into the mountains."

## 1935–1938

Freer's experiences on the Bedaux Expedition gave him important skills,

Willard and Jack MacDougall sawing a deer roast near Hudson's Hope in 1935. Bob White Family collection

developed his confidence, and motivated him to move to the wilderness area of the Finlay River. Freer returned to Hudson's Hope, and probably in 1936, he began life as a trapper in the Ingenika River valley near the Hudson's Bay Company post at Fort Grahame. The area where he trapped was near Shorty Weber's. (Weber had been arrested a few times for crimes and once was a suspect for a murder.) Freer's trapline was not officially registered with the BC government until 1940.

## 1939—PRELIMINARY ALASKA HIGHWAY SURVEY

The threat of another world war became more imminent in 1939. Although British Columbia seemed far away from events in Europe, the province provided the main land connection between the United States and its territory in Alaska. If there was a war, the United States would want a road constructed to Alaska through British Columbia.

The idea of an Alaska Highway had started in the late 1920s, and in 1930, the BC government made a major survey for a route that largely followed present day Highway 37 (Stewart-Cassiar Highway). British Columbia's surveyor general, F.C. Green, was a strong advocate for an Alaska Highway, but the Depression prevented development. In 1939, with economic conditions improving and a world war seeming more likely, the British Columbia government hired several crews to make a preliminary highway survey. Green favoured a highway that would run north from Prince George through the Rocky Mountain Trench to Lower Post near the Yukon border

Freer (right) and Count Nicholas Ignatieff. The Count, a teacher at Upper Canada College in Toronto, came to northern BC for many summers, and eventually purchased land in the area. The Ignatieff family fled Russia after the Communist Revolution. He is the uncle of Michael Ignatieff, leader of the Liberal Party from 2009 to 2011, when he lost the federal election. E008222046, Library and Archives Canada.

because it would be the shortest route and the easiest to construct.

The northern Rocky Mountain Trench became the site of considerable activity in 1939. The Department of Public Works hired two surveyors to conduct reconnaissance work, examining the potential route for the highway and noting any possible difficulties. The Forestry Branch assigned Gerry Andrews, in charge of aerial photography for the province, to make a set of aerial photographs of the Rocky Mountain Trench from Finlay Forks to Sifton Pass.

The Survey Branch of the BC government had four phototopographic survey crews mapping the area. In addition, two triangulation surveying crews worked in the Rocky Mountain Trench from the Ingenika River through the Kechika River valley north of Sifton Pass. Frank Swannell was in charge of the triangulation survey crew working from the Ingenika River to Sifton Pass, while Hugh Pattinson surveyed in the Kechika River valley. Both Swannell and Pattinson had been on the PGE Resources survey in 1929 and 1930 in the Peace River district, and Swannell's 1930 surveying had finished by the Ingenika River.

Swannell had a veteran crew in 1939. It included the famous packer, John Ogilvie "Skook" Davidson, who transported men and goods for both Swannell's and Pattinson's crews. Much of Swannell's work was along the Finlay River, and he mainly used boat transportation until he reached the Fox River, so Skook worked primarily with Pattinson's crew. Swannell also hired Freer, who lived in the area where he was going to survey. Although the two men had been on different sections of the Bedaux Expedition, they had had an opportunity to become acquainted during the last month of the 1934 adventure.

The BC government purchased two freight boats for Swannell to use while surveying on the Finlay River. Freer joined Swannell's crew when they arrived in mid-June. The men camped at Swannell's 1930 campsite at the mouth of the Ingenika River and then moved up to Deserters Canyon. The water was too high and swift to navigate the canyon, so Swannell's men had to portage the boats and supplies.

Swannell split his crew into two groups. He placed his assistant, Thorne Forrest, BCLS (British Columbia Land Surveyor) #258, in charge of a group that surveyed from the peaks along the Rocky Mountain Trench. Freer was with Forrest. Meanwhile, Swannell connected his 1930 surveying with his 1939 work and set survey stations up to Deserters Canyon.

Swannell's crew reached Fort Ware by the end of July. On the last day of the month, Forrest, Freer and packer Ron Campbell left on a trip to set stations up the Rocky Mountain Trench toward Sifton Pass. Meanwhile, Swannell and his men surveyed around Fort Ware and the area where the Finlay left the Rocky Mountain Trench. They then proceeded up the trench, connecting their work to the stations Forrest set on the peaks.

Forrest's group rejoined the crew on August 17. During the next two weeks, Swannell surveyed toward Sifton Pass. His assistant, Al Phipps, and Walter Nehring went to the pass and surveyed from Pattinson's first two stations, connecting them with Swannell's work.

On September 1, Swannell surveyed at some stations around Weissener Lake southeast of Sifton Pass. He had a radio with him, so he heard about Germany's invasion of Poland and the beginning of World War II that day. Two days later Britain declared war, and by then Phipps and Nehring had returned from Sifton Pass. Although there was about a month left to the field season, Swannell had completed his main objectives, and he felt that he should return to Victoria, for Canada would soon be involved in the war. It took about ten days for Swannell to finish a small amount of surveying and take all the men and equipment back. Since Pattinson's crew was farther away and had more work remaining, it stayed in the field until later in September.

By the end of the 1939 field season, Hugh Pattinson had only surveyed part of the Kechika River valley, and he anticipated returning in 1940. Pattinson received permission from the BC government to pay Skook to winter their horses in the Kechika River valley. This provided Skook with income for the winter along with an opportunity to develop his own ranch, something he had wanted to do for many years. During the summer, he examined the Kechika River valley. Despite its northern latitude and remote location, Skook thought that the valley provided good habitat for horses. The west-facing slopes on the east side of the valley would provide good feed, and the snow would melt early in the spring. He heard that the valley did not get a large amount of rain, and snowfall was usually light. He also learned that there were spells of very cold weather in the winter, but they did not last long before warm southern and western winds came into the valley. At the end of the summer, while others were returning to their homes, Skook headed north to begin a new phase of his illustrious career as a packer.

During the summer of 1939, Freer would have had an opportunity to meet Skook, and that connection would impact the lives of both men a few years later.

## Skook Davidson

John Ogilvie "Skook" Davidson is one of British Columbia's most famous and colourful outdoorsmen. Born in 1892 in Scotland, he came to Canada as a ship's boy when he was thirteen. He travelled to the Cariboo region of British Columbia where he learned how to be a packer from the famous Jean Caux (known as Cataline).

In June 1916, Skook enlisted in World War I, serving until the spring of 1919. He was involved in several battles and received the Military Medal with two bars and the Distinguished Conduct Medal.

After returning from the war, Skook moved north to Fort St. James. From there he packed supplies to the mining camps in the Omineca district farther north. Much of his work was for Bob and Bert McCorkell, Americans who operated placer mines there. McCorkell also took hunting trips north from his Cassiar Ranch near Fort St. James. Skook worked on contract for McCorkell as a packer for many of his trips.

Skook Davidson at the end of the 1939 field season, preparing to spend his first winter in the Kechika River valley. E008222047, Library and Archives Canada

In the field seasons of 1929, 1930 and 1931, Skook was packer and boatman for the famous BC surveyor Frank Swannell.

In 1939, Skook was hired by Frank Swannell to be the packer for his crew and for Pattinson's, the two triangulation survey crews working on the preliminary route for a road north from Prince George to Alaska via the Rocky Mountain Trench. Most of Swannell's work was accessible by boat along the Finlay River, so most of Skook's packing was for Pattinson's crew.

Fred and Annie Forsberg were among Skook's first visitors. This was Skook's first cabin at the site of his Diamond J Ranch. Image I-68945 courtesy the Royal BC Museum and Archives

Home Ranch in the 1960s with Terminus Mountain, the northernmost peak in the Rockies, in the background. Skook Davidson Family collection

Since the BC government intended to continue surveying north down the Kechika River in 1940, Skook built a small cabin over the winter of 1939–40 and established the Diamond J Ranch along Metulka Creek close to the Kechika River. This became Skook's home until a fire in 1972 destroyed most of the ranch buildings. Skook, who was in poor health at that time, then sold the ranch and moved to a nursing home in North Vancouver where he died in 1977.

Home place on the Ingenika. Willard Freer Family collection

## 1939–1941

Jack Blanchard, a trapper and miner who had a cabin along the Finlay River near Finlay Forks, was a member of Swannell's crew for part of the 1939 surveying season. Freer must have made an arrangement with Blanchard, for there is a letter from Blanchard written in 1939 in the BC government's correspondence file giving Freer permission to trap on his line. In 1940, Freer registered a trapline along the Ingenika River near its intersection with the Pelly that included territory both south and north of the Ingenika.

Freer was at his main trapline cabin when his surviving diaries begin, on April 1, 1942.

Fleshing beaver. 2003.15.124b, Mackenzie Museum

# THE 1940S: 1942–1949

## HIGHLIGHTS

The United States entered World War II after Japan bombed the American base at Pearl Harbor in Hawaii in late 1941. For the Americans, it was imperative that there be an all-weather road that connected the continental United States with its territory in Alaska. The construction of the Alaska Highway had profound effects on the people of northern British Columbia that continued after the conclusion of the war.

In 1942, Freer came to the Kechika River valley. He stayed at the Diamond J Ranch belonging to the famous packer, Skook Davidson, and worked for him for the remainder of the decade.

Skook and Freer started a trading store at the ranch in 1945, where they bartered food and supplies for fur with the Indigenous trappers of the Kechika River valley during the winter and early spring. This store had a large impact on the economy and ecology of the area.

This decade was the high watermark for horse pack trains in northern BC. From 1942 to 1949, Freer had a packing job every summer. Six of the summers were spent on government survey crews (provincial, federal, and interestingly, a summer with the United States Army) in northern BC. The other two summers were spent with Consolidated Mining and Smelting (CM&S), one of the major mining companies in British Columbia at that time.

## 1942

*April 1–May 30 Trapping cabin along the Ingenika River*

> *April 1* "I finished hauling the wood that I had on the Ingenika River ice at noon. The ice is getting rotten. I put a sort of bridge across a back slough and broke a trail out to where I have some more wood to haul yet. The snow is very soft and warm, strong chinook wind after dinner. It was very cloudy all day."

On Freer's birthday, April 19, he trapped the first beaver.

> *April 23* "The damn beaver aren't moving at all."

> *April 29* "The god damn beaver aren't moving at all."

*May 2* "I went down Wrede Creek and brought back 3 beaver, two extra-large and one large. I skinned all and stretched one. I have traps down about 5 miles [8 kilometres]. I made a beaver stretcher out of hewed boards."

Rising water ended beaver trapping on May 17.

### *May 30–June 16 Finlay River area*

Freer sold furs to the HBC at Fort Grahame and helped portage supplies through Deserters Canyon for Del Miller and priest.

### *June 17– October 13 Employed with the United States Army in Northern BC*

Initially Freer was employed at Deserters Canyon "as watchman as there is about 10 tons [9,080 kilograms] of supplies here in caches."

*June 25* Freer arrived at Fort Ware. "There is sure a bunch of men at Ware on the US survey."

At Fort Ware, Willard and Skook went to work immediately packing outfits and transporting survey crews, for Major Charles wanted to start surveying north of Fort Ware as soon as possible. By July 3, the entire survey crew was at the 12 Mile camp near the junction of the Finlay and Fox Rivers.

*July 13* Freer "took Maj. Charles and C.H. Davis to 17 mile where Skook and party are building rafts. John Rasmussen and I took Charles and Davis down the Fox River to Davis' fly camp on the Fox.… We sure had lots of fun coming down the Fox."

The next day Skook took Major Charles to Fort Ware.

*July 14* "Maj. Charles is going to check over the other parties on the Finlay."

The surveying proceeded smoothly through the summer as the crew and packers proceeded north toward Sifton Pass.

On September 15, the return trip to Fort Ware started, and a week later the survey crew was back in Fort Ware. Freer went to join Party 5 at Fox Pass and stayed with this survey crew as they completed their work and moved back toward Fort Ware.

*Oct 9* "Johnny Rasmussen came out with orders from Major Charles to quit the job. All the men are happy now."

*Oct 11* "We laid around all day and did nothing. No excitement at all. Well, all the parties are finished and thank God for small mercies."

## Major John Leslie Charles and the Trans-Canadian Alaskan Railway Survey

During 1942, Willard Freer and several people in northern BC had the unique distinction of working for the United States Army.

After the American naval base at Pearl Harbor in Hawaii was bombed, the Allied countries (including Canada) declared war on Japan in December 1941. The situation made the need for a secure land link between the United States and its Alaska territory paramount. In addition to constructing a highway through British Columbia, the United States decided to explore the possibility of building a railway. It would follow the same route as the BC government's 1939 highway survey. The project, which was called the Trans-Canadian Alaska Railway survey, was initiated in March 1942.

On April 22, 1942, Canada's Secretary of State for External Affairs wrote to the United States Minister to Canada.

> … the Canadian government, while doubting the practicability of the proposal to construct a railway from Prince George to Fairbanks at the present time when manpower, equipment and steel are all in short supply, is prepared to agree to the carrying out of a survey of the route of the proposed line by agencies of the United States government. It is, of course, understood that this agreement does not in any way commit the Canadian government to approval of the proposed construction.

The secretary reminded the minister that the "road surveys carried out by the British Columbia-Yukon-Alaska Commission cover much the same territory as that which is of interest to the proponents of the railway scheme, and that use of these surveys should greatly assist in reducing the labours of those engaged on the railway survey."

On April 28, Henry L. Stimson, United States secretary of war, wrote to the secretary of state:

> The Chief of Engineers has requested that arrangements be made for the detail of Major John L. Charles… for duty with the U.S. Army.… Major Charles is a qualified railroad locating engineer familiar with the Northwest and particularly that section of British Columbia through which the proposed route will pass and his services would be of great assistance in conducting the survey.
>
> It is therefore respectfully requested that the Secretary of State initiate action with a view to securing the permission of the Canadian government for the detail of Major Charles to duty

with the U.S. Army as assistant to the District Engineer at Seattle for the remainder of the year.

Charles had been the chief engineer for the Canadian National Railway in western Canada. He also served in World War I and World War II.

During the 1942 field season, Charles had several survey parties in the field, most of them on the section from Fort Ware to Lower Post. The logistics for moving the crews was handled by local boatmen, packers and trappers, according to Charles. One of them was Skook Davidson. Famous bush pilot Russ Baker had a Junkers airplane that Charles used occasionally for flights.

Initially the project was kept secret, but in a July 9, 1942, article the *Prince George Citizen* stated: "Apparently satisfied with preliminary findings and development, the United States War Department has advanced into the open sufficiently to announce that the army has surveyed about one-third of a proposed railway route to Alaska to supplement the inland highway under construction."

Major Charles submitted his report by the end of October. In his report on the British Columbia section, Charles found no major impediments to the BC section of the proposed Trans-Canadian Alaska Railway.

On November 15, US General Brehon Somervell declined to proceed with a military railway because of the expense and the time it would take to construct a rail line. He believed that the considerable progress made on the construction of the Alaska Highway in 1942, along with the limitation of the Japanese army to the Aleutian Islands in North America, made the construction of a railway unnecessary.

## October 13–December 31 Kechika River and Diamond J Ranch

Freer made a decision that would impact the rest of his life. He was going to follow the wilderness to one of the most remote regions of British Columbia.

*Oct 13* At Fort Ware: "Craig Forfar came in on the plane from Fort St. James. He is going to winter in with Skook Davidson. I am going to winter there too."

*Oct 15* "We fixed up our loads and will pull out tomorrow for Gataga Forks on the Big Muddy [Kechika] River."

*Oct 16* The journey to Skook's ranch started. "Johnny Rasmussen, Craig Forfar and I left Fort Ware for Skook Davidson's home range. Skook is along. We are heavily loaded. We made 12 mile camp at 6 PM. The loads all rode good."

Craig Forfar was fifteen years old. His father, Ed, had been a BC Provincial Police constable in the Peace River district in the early 1920s. Then he became a guide and hotel proprietor at Fort St. James for many years, and he knew Skook well. Ed committed suicide in January 1940, and Craig's mother, Molly, remarried six months later. She arranged for Skook to care for her son.

The group arrived at Skook's Diamond J Ranch on October 29. Skook needed to expand his cabin, so during early November the men hauled logs and dug a cellar. On November 8, they started to frame the addition.

> *Nov 11* "We finished the walls of cabin, got all the split poles on, and started to cut the windows."

> *Nov 20* "We finished up the kitchen and moved everything in. We had our first meal in there." Freer made a bunk in the cabin and moved out of the tent on November 23.

Skook, John Rasmussen and John Bergman departed for Fort Ware on December 11. Skook had confidence in Freer's ability to manage the ranch, with Forfar to assist him. This enabled Skook to leave the Diamond J for an extended period, although it became much longer than originally planned.

Daily life at the ranch was quiet for Freer and Forfar. There were basic chores to be done. The most important thing was to ensure that the horses remained healthy and safe, particularly the mares and colts. Freer did the cooking and indoor chores, while Forfar did most of the outdoor work. Both men spent time looking after the horses.

On December 18, Jack Abou and his partner came from the Turnagain River and stayed overnight. Abou was one of the first Indigenous people with whom Freer had considerable contact.

> *Dec 30* "Fred Forsberg came by here along with his wife Annie.... Fred and wife haven't eaten for two days."

Fred was a trapper, and Annie was a member of the McCook family. The Forsberg trapline was in the Rabbit River drainage to the east of the Kechika and was part of the McCook traditional territory. During his first years at the Diamond J, Freer met Fred and Annie occasionally.

# 1943

## *January 1–May 19 Diamond J Ranch with Craig Forfar*

Freer's main responsibility was caring for horses. A few visitors came to the ranch. In late February, Freer heard that Skook had gone to Prince George. (Skook, who became a special constable for the BC Provincial Police around

1940, took an assignment to arrest Steven Poole, a person accused of murder at Fort Ware.)

> *Mar 11* "John Rasmussen arrived from Fort Ware and brought news that Skook Davidson went to Jim Beattie's at Hudson Hope to buy more horses." This was the beginning of Skook's own herd of horses.

## "REX VS. POOLE, STEPHEN (MURDER)"

The murder of Margaret Poole by her husband Steven at Fort Ware on January 8, 1943, received considerable coverage in the *Prince George Citizen* newspaper. It was summarized in the BC Sessional Papers and is also described in *BC Provincial Police Stories: Volume Three*.

Steven claimed that his wife had frozen to death after drinking alcohol at a party, but several people did not believe this explanation and the BC Provincial Police were contacted. Because of weather conditions, the police were unable to get to Fort Ware until February 4, twenty-four days after receiving the news. Meanwhile, Poole buried his wife and went to his trapline. Skook Davidson, who was a special constable, arrived in Fort Ware with the police. At their request, Skook remained and arrested Poole when he returned to Fort Ware on March 2. The personnel necessary for the inquest quickly flew from Prince George to Fort Ware, and Margaret Poole's body was exhumed for the proceedings, held on March 3.

"Police party getting on plane at Fort Ware. Rex vs. Steve Poole, murder." Image B-06171 courtesy the Royal BC Museum and Archives

BC Provincial Police Stories described the scene at Fort Ware that evening. Around midnight four men reburied Margaret under a moonlit sky. Skook decided to give her a "soldier's farewell." "He drew his gun and solemnly fired six shots in the air.... From the pocket of his pea jacket, Sergeant Clark produced a mickey of rum. Wordlessly it passed from hand to hand to quick extinction. Turning from the mound of earth, slowly and silently the quartet plodded down over the snow-covered trail to the river. As they did so, far back in the foothills a timber wolf mournfully howled for its mate. 'Requiem for Margaret Poole', was Clark's comment."

A front-page article in the March 4 *Prince George Citizen* stated: "Steven Poole of the Beaver Indian tribe at Fort Ware has been charged with murder following an inquest and preliminary hearing held at Fort Ware Wednesday. Poole's 25-year-old wife Margaret Poole was found on the night of January 8 on the ice of Finlay River with her head crushed with blows from a rifle. The accused man was brought to Prince George jail Thursday by airplane."

The trial was initially scheduled for May but was "set over when witnesses not present." In early October, a two-day trial was held. The *Prince George Citizen* had a front-page headline on October 7: *Poole Guilty Manslaughter; Sentenced to Life in Prison* with a sub-headline: "Jury finds Fort Ware Native guilty of slaying wife on January 8 last—Tragedy follows drinking party at lonely northern outpost—accused denies knowledge of crime."

The newspaper provided a detailed account of the trial:

> Star witness for the prosecution… was Tommy Poole, 11-year-old son of the accused, who said he had seen his father club his mother with a rifle on the Finlay River the night of January 8 and then take off her dress and hid it in the ice.
>
> The boy also testified the father later at the family cabin struck him across the forehead and nose with the rifle. Poole told his son the mother was dead and ordered him to say nothing to his grandmother.
>
> Later, the young witness said, he went to his mother and covered her with his sweater.

Del Miller noted the wound when he and Charles Van Somer visited Steven Poole on January 10. During this same visit, Miller and Van Somer saw the body of Margaret Poole. "The woman's face was black and blue," testified Miller, and he told Poole: "It looks like she has been clubbed to death."

Steven maintained his innocence, but the jury pronounced him guilty of manslaughter in ninety minutes.

The construction of the Alaska Highway, which began in 1942, had profound effects on the Indigenous people of northern BC and Yukon. Freer's diary entries for May 7 and 8 describe some of the ways their lives changed.

> *May 7* "I had lunch and started to look up the horses. Got as far as the meadow, met Fred and Annie Forsberg coming from Lower Post. They were sick for 12 days. Everybody is sick at Lower Post. Quite a few people dying from the influenza. They report that everything is booming at Lower Post and Watson Lake on the Alaska Highway. They report that fur prices are very good. They report a very bad trip from Lower Post."

> *May 8* "Donald [McCook] reports quite a few Indians dying at Fort Ware and lots sick too. There seems to be a sort of flu going around. Donald returned to Gataga River after dinner."

*May 19–30 Trip to Fort Ware*

*May 30–June 18 At Fort Ware, preparing for trip to surveying location and waiting for Skook Davidson to arrive with horses purchased from Jim Beattie*

Willard was assistant packer and Skook was head packer for the BC government triangulation survey being made by Hugh Pattinson in northwestern BC. Twenty-five horses were used for transportation because the remote location of the work made it necessary to take all their food and supplies for the summer with them. The poor condition of the trails made travel difficult.

## HUGH PATTINSON

Hugh Pattinson, BCLS #233, worked on surveying projects for the BC government in the northern part of the province for several years. His triangulation mapping survey of northwestern British Columbia, which started in 1939, continued throughout World War II. In 1940, he returned to the Kechika River valley, hiring Skook as his packer again, and using the horses he had left with Skook during the winter. Pattinson surveyed north down the Kechika to the Turnagain River, the main tributary of the Kechika on the west side, where he connected to a government survey made by Philip Monckton the previous year. From the Turnagain, Pattinson surveyed toward Dease Lake to the southwest.

After finishing in the Dease Lake area, Pattinson primarily surveyed in the upper Stikine watershed during 1941 and 1942. For both years he used Telegraph Creek as his base of operations. Pattinson's last station in 1942 was in a very remote location where the headwaters of northwestern BC's three great rivers, the Stikine, Nass, and Skeena, are in close proximity.

In his government report for 1943, Pattinson wrote: "During the season at least 50 miles [80 kilometres] of old trail were brushed out and sufficient windfalls removed to make pack horse travel possible…. When moving camp it was customary to have two or three men ahead of the pack train with axes and machetes, reblazing and brushing out the old trails so there would be as little delay as possible."

In 1944 and 1945, Pattinson completed this government surveying project by basing his operations out of Fort St. James and surveying in the headwaters of the Skeena and Stuart Rivers.

### June 18–July 13 Travel to surveying location

Surveyor Hugh Pattinson described the journey at the beginning of the season in his BC government report.

On June 18 the party commenced the long trail trip to Kluayaz Lake in the valley of the Kluatantan River, in the vicinity of which the first stations to be occupied was located…. From Caribou Hide a route was taken following Laslui, Tuaton and Happy Lakes to the extreme head of the Stikine River, then over a timberline pass and down Skelhorne Creek to the Kluatantan-Kluayetz; whence an existing trail was followed to our first main camp in the vicinity of Kluayaz Lake. Work started July 15.

### July 15–August 17 Taking care of base camp while survey crews in field

### August 17–26 All crews working together

All the men joined together on August 17. They made camp about three kilometres up Malloch Creek where they spent three days because several men were sick.

### August 27–October 23 Return trips

Freer made a round trip between Fort Ware and the Diamond J Ranch from September 9 to October 7 and remained at Fort Ware until October 12.

*Oct 11* "A new HBC manager came by, name Charles Hamilton. Bill Gorman and family went out. Del Miller, Art van Somers and family were on the plane coming back from Pat Poole's trial. He was sentenced to life imprisonment."

Freer returned to Skook's ranch on October 23.

*October 23–December 31 Diamond J Ranch*

*Dec 30* "I started to Davie Creek to look after the horses. Met Fred and Annie Forsberg just coming from their trap line at Horn Lake. They report a scarcity of fresh meat, but plenty of fur. I returned to home from the lake." On the last day of the year, the three of them "did nothing all day, just laid around."

# 1944

*January 1–May 27 Diamond J Ranch*

In late April, Freer made an unsuccessful trip to Fort Ware to see if he could find information about summer work.

*May 19* Francis Charlie arrived with the mail. "I am to report for work at Lower Post June 5 [19]44 with 10 head of horses." Freer would be the packer for C.H. Ney of the Dominion Geodetic Survey.

## C.H. NEY AND THE DOMINION GEODETIC SURVEY

The 60th parallel was established as the northern boundary of British Columbia in 1863. Most of this 1,056-kilometre boundary is shared with Yukon Territory; a small portion of the eastern section has a common boundary with Northwest Territories. British Columbia's land is administered by the provincial government, while Yukon and Northwest Territories are handled by the federal government.

The first survey of the BC-Yukon Territory boundary occurred at the end of the nineteenth century, when the Klondike Gold Rush made delineation of the 60th parallel important for administrative purposes. From 1899 to 1908, the BC-Yukon boundary was surveyed between Tatshenshini River and Teslin Lake.

The route selected for the Alaska Highway in 1942 crosses and recrosses the 60th parallel a few times, and it runs close to the BC-Yukon

Cornice station. Land Title & Survey Authority of BC (LTSA)

boundary for many kilometres. It became imperative to resume surveying and define the boundary east from Teslin Lake to the vicinity of the Smith River.

In 1943 the BC government and the federal government established a British Columbia-Yukon-Northwest Territories Boundary Commission. The costs for the survey would be shared equally by the federal and BC governments.

The Boundary Commission report stated that the principle employed for establishing the 60th parallel was the same as that used in delineating the 49th parallel, which defined part of Canada's border with the United States. "The first step, therefore, in the determination of the boundary was the establishment of astronomically fixed control points or astrofixes."

The Boundary Commission listed four specific requirements for the surveying of each astrofix. The commission also wanted longitude observations at each astrofix, stating that "these were desirable for map control but not essential for the boundary survey." The distance between each astrofix was to be approximately twenty-four kilometres.

The federal Geodetic Service had high-quality surveying equipment and trained surveyors for this precise work. In 1943, J.E.R. Ross established five astrofixes (R1–R5) close to where the 60th parallel crossed the newly completed Alaska Highway. In 1944, the Geodetic Service sent C.H. Ney, a veteran surveyor who had worked in the remote Arctic for many years. He was instructed "to make additional [astro]fixes between those made by Ross to conform with the precedent established on the 49th parallel where astrofixes were spaced at intervals of about 15 miles [24 kilometres]." Ney established five intermediate astrofixes, N1–N5, along with another astrofix, N6, which was farther east at Smith River. N6 is about sixty-four kilometres east of the last crossing of the Alaska Highway and was at the end of the section of the 60th parallel that the Boundary Commission intended to survey at that time. Ney also had to accurately determine the latitude of the astrofixes he established, for they would be the basis for determining the survey line defining this section of the BC-Yukon boundary.

After the establishment of these astrofixes, the actual surveying of the 60th parallel started in 1945 and continued until 1949. The survey of the boundary resumed in 1952 because the discovery of petroleum and natural gas near the 60th parallel made it imperative to complete the eastern part of BC's northern boundary.

### *May 27–June 6 Travel to Lower Post*

### *June 6–18 Waiting for C.H. Ney*

> *June 3* "Arrived at the Dease River landing across the river from Lower Post. Charlie Porter's camped here."

> *June 6* "Swam the horses across the Dease and Liard Rivers to north side. Fred Forsberg helped me. Lots of trucks and cars here on the Alaska Highway."

> *June 13* "The trappers still coming in. Laid around all day. The Lake boat came in from Dease Lake."

Ney kept a diary for the 1944 field season that describes his trip to Lower Post. Leaving Ottawa on June 4, he travelled on the Canadian National Railway train to Edmonton. When he arrived there three days later, it took four days to hire a cook and an additional labourer. On June 11, Ney left for Dawson Creek at 5:30 p.m., arriving there twenty-four hours later. He spent a couple of days making necessary arrangements, including obtaining permits to enter the Alaska Highway and to buy gas and oil along the route. (The Alaska Highway was a military road during World War II and civilians had to obtain permits to travel the route.) Ney left for Lower Post on June 15. Three days later, he stopped at Liard Hot Springs, before arriving at Lower Post at 2:00 p.m. where he "found packer and ten horses waiting."

### *June 19–August 28 Astrofix survey*

Freer was packer for the Dominion Government's astrofix survey, work preliminary to the resumption of the British Columbia-Yukon Boundary Survey of the 60th parallel. The survey started over two hundred kilometres west of Lower Post. Freer noted that it was cooler for the horses to travel in the evening, and they weren't distracted by traffic on the highway.

*August 28–September 7 Lower Post*

*September 7–September 24 Return trip to Diamond J Ranch*

Freer reached the Kechika on September 13, where heavy rain delayed his crossing.

> *Sept 18* "I made a raft here and it rained hard, clearing towards evening. North wind. Looks as though never going to quit raining."

> *Sept 21* "I swam the horses, had a hell of a job by myself."

Freer finally arrived at the ranch on September 24.

*September 28–October 21 Fort Ware trip*

Skook, Frank Cooke Jr. and Freer made a trip to Fort Ware to pick up grub and machinery. This equipment had been left at Moose Valley after Bedaux's failed attempt to establish a ranch in 1935 and 1936. Skook and Frank Cooke Jr. took the machinery to Fort Ware in the summer of 1944. The return trip took twelve days because the horses were packing heavy, awkward items like plows and sleighs that had been dismantled.

*October 22–December 31 Diamond J Ranch*

> *Dec 31* "Old McCook [Mac] and Jack Abou came down from Gataga River."

In 1944, Skook Davidson decided to get a Class A guiding licence. He probably realized that after Pattinson's survey and the BC-Yukon boundary were completed there would likely be no more large surveying projects in the area. Skook was the first Class A guide in the Kechika valley. Taking guided trips from the Diamond J Ranch would provide income and utilize his horses. Although he got his licence, Skook did not use it for a few years. Nevertheless, the provincial government maintained it. J.W. Stewart, the game warden for the Lower Post detachment, wrote a letter to the commanding officer of the Game Department in Prince George on July 31, 1948.

> In the Lower Post Detachment we have had only two guides: J.O. Davidson, who I believe is entitled to a first class guide licence; George Edzerza, an Indian, who had his first licence last year. I also have an application from Tom Harvey, Lower Post, who has been here for ten years, and

has a small pack outfit, also one from Fred Forsberg who is one of our trappers and will be employed by J.O. Davidson who is taking the Pop party out in the Muddy River area this year.

The Prince George detachment replied:

"Re the above, as you have no 'overcrowding' of guides in your area, it will be in order for you to issue a few Class 2 licences, to applicants who have never held licences previously and to ones who have held one licence."

Skook's guiding licence would eventually impact the Kechika valley and its residents. Hunting trips brought visitors to the area, created seasonal employment for some of the local inhabitants, and led to more guides working in the Kechika valley and surrounding area.

Freer at Fort Ware. Willard Freer Family collection

# 1945

*January 1–May 26 Diamond J Ranch*

> *Jan 29* "3 Indian dog teams went down river to Lower Post: Donald McCook and wife; Perry Massetoe; and one of the George boys. Jack Abou and John McCook went back to City Cabins. I strung up the new aerial." Like many people

living in the remote areas of BC, Skook had a radio set for communication with the outside world.

## May 26–June 1 Trip to Fort Ware

"Travel en route to Thutade Lake. Stayed one day."

## June 3–7 Trip to Thutade Lake

Freer had obtained summer employment as packer for Emil Bronlund, prominent mining engineer for Consolidated Mining and Smelting (CM&S).

### EMIL BRONLUND

Bronlund (1896–1988) was born in Norway and obtained a bachelor of science in mining and metallurgical engineering from the University of Oslo before immigrating to Canada in 1920. Initially he was an engineer for a coal mine near Hinton, Alberta, and at the Ingenika Mine in northern BC. In 1927 Consolidated Mining and Smelting (later Cominco and Teck Resources) hired Bronlund to be in charge of their mineral exploration in northern BC, a position he held for almost twenty-five years. Most of his work was in the Omineca district north of Fort St. James.

In an obituary for Bronlund, the *Northern Miner*, a trade journal, commented that "Bronlund was a member of Cominco's flying corps of prospectors which did much to open up the north in the 1930s." The journal also noted that "several properties in the Omineca district now under development are his original finds." During World War II, Bronlund was Consolidated's manager for the Pinchi Lake mercury mine northwest of Fort St. James. It was the largest producer of mercury in the country at that time.

Bronlund Peak and Bronlund Creek in northern BC are named for him.

## June 7–October 5 Thutade Lake

Freer's main job was to pack equipment and supplies to the location where the men were working. He also went hunting and fishing.

> *Aug 6* "E. Bronlund and I went up Thutade Lake and camped on Attichika Creek about 4 miles [6.4 kilometres] up the creek from Thutade Lake. Trail not bad. George Meyers put us across Thutade Lake."

> *Aug 7–8* Bronlund spent the two days prospecting while Freer tended camp and did the cooking.

*Aug 9* The two men returned to the main camp. Freer wrote: "Bronlund is quite sick."

*Sept 12* A plane arrived with mail. Unfortunately, "All our mail went to Uslika Lake and we got Ruby mail here."

*Oct 5* Freer departed from Thutade Lake. "George Meyers and E. Bronlund helped to swim the lake. I made about 6 miles [9.6 kilometres]. Snowed all afternoon."

*October 5–12 Trip to Fort Ware; stayed one day*

*October 14–26 Return trip to Diamond J Ranch*

*Oct 14* "I have 8 packs. Am headed for the home range, Muddy River."

*Oct 18* "Thank goodness, am on the north side of Sifton Pass again."

*October 27–December 31 Diamond J Ranch*

In the back of Freer's 1945–46 diary, there is a record of fur trade licence #5805. When Skook returned from the British Columbia-Yukon Boundary Survey in the fall of 1945, he had several packhorses with him. At Lower Post, he purchased food and supplies to take back to the Kechika valley. Skook had decided to establish an unofficial trading post where he would exchange goods for furs and occasionally other items.

Previously, for the inhabitants of the Kechika valley, the Hudson's Bay Company posts at Fort Ware on the Finlay River and Lower Post on the Liard River were their main trade centres. After World War II, it was inevitable that the Alaska Highway would become a main transportation route in northern BC. Food and supplies became available year-round and were less expensive when they were shipped by truck on the Alaska Highway. There was also a large airport at nearby Watson Lake in Yukon Territory that was constructed during World War II. From there, planes could fly into the Kechika valley in less than an hour. For most of the inhabitants of the valley, the economic base switched from Fort Ware, initially to Lower Post, and then to Watson Lake. This change began after the war ended and accelerated after the Alaska Highway opened to the public in 1948.

The 1945 provincial game warden's report for D Division (which included the Kechika valley) stated: "Fur trade in general benefitted from an increase in prices and a greater number of traders entered the field, and old-established traders extended the scope of their enterprises by establishing posts at various points in the Division, resulting in better prices being paid to the trapper. An even better season is anticipated for the next year." There was also a note: "A great deal of the fur-take in this district is sold directly to buyers in Vancouver."

Skook's trading arrangements produced important changes in the economy of the Kechika valley for many of its inhabitants. Previously a trip to Lower Post or Fort Ware would take several days for most people, so they would only go to the trading posts a couple of times each year. One of these trips would usually be made in the spring after trapping had finished. The furs would be sold for goods, which would have to be transported back to their residences. With Skook's trading system, people could come to the Diamond J whenever they acquired some furs and immediately exchange them for goods. This provided the valley's residents with certainty regarding the price they would receive for their furs along with a greater choice of food and other supplies during the winter. Skook had a good sense of the value of the furs and the amount of supplies that he could trade that would be agreeable to the local people yet eventually produce a profit for him.

Skook's clientele were mainly people who lived in the Kechika drainage within two days of travel. Almost all these people had accounts with Skook for more than one trapping season. Skook or his helpers put up a large tent with a wood stove near the ranch every winter for the Indigenous inhabitants to use, which helped facilitate the trading.

Skook's ledger journal from October 1945 to April 1948 was donated by Gord Yule, a great-nephew of Skook, to the Northern BC Archives (NBCA) in 2021. The NBCA intends to post a copy on its website.

Skook listed each item that a person purchased and its cost. He also recorded any credit or debt that a person had. The credit was usually for furs, but sometimes it was wages for work on the ranch. Skook often, but not always, listed the species of fur he acquired. Skook's ledger begins on October 29, 1945, "in account with Diamond J pack train." His first entries are for Jimmy and Michel McCook. The two McCooks had worked for Skook and had $200 in credit. They purchased over $300 of food.

The ledger journal documents the economic activity of the inhabitants of the Kechika valley, especially trapping. It also shows spending habits and differences in approach to Skook's unofficial trading store.

Freer's diaries frequently correlate with Skook's ledger journal to provide detail about the activities of the valley's residents.

> *Oct 29* Freer wrote that he, Skook and Michel McCook "went to Davie Creek and came back with 7 head of horses packed. John and Jim came up."

*Oct 30* "Skook got 6 loads of grub ready for Jim and Michel McCook who are staying and trapping from City Cabins. They have been packing with Skook all summer on the BC-Yukon boundary survey."

*Oct 31* Freer "packed Michel and Jim McCook's winter grub stake to Gataga Forks. John McCook went up too and is on his way to Fort Ware. I saw Joe and Fred McCook at Gataga River. Had up 8 horse loads." Joe's ledger account showed that he purchased a small amount of goods, while John had a $100 credit for a month of wages.

*Nov 1* "Returned home from Gataga River with the eight horses. Louie and Joe Boya and Frank Stone came from Horn Creek." All three men purchased supplies.

*Nov 2* "Skook and I went to Davie Creek. Skook brought home four horse loads of grub. Louie Boya, Joe Boya and Frank Stone were here. They went to Horn Creek."

More diary entries in November and December document continual trading activity. Skook and Freer went to Davie Creek on November 9 to pick up four more loads of supplies, and this trip was repeated several times.

*Nov 23* "Joe and Charlie Boya came up and returned to Horn Creek. Skook and I took the four head of horses and packed up more grub from Davie Creek."

*Dec 12* "Skook and I went to Davie Creek and returned with the big cook stove. Amos Alec, Felix Johnnie, Louie Boya, Joe Boya came up from Turnagain River." They purchased over $100 of food and supplies. Alec received a $50 credit for beaver he had trapped and had a credit of $27 after his purchases. Johnnie got $37 for a mink and fisher which almost covered the cost of the items he selected. Louie Boya's purchases totaled $63.50.

In the following days, some of the Indigenous inhabitants visited Freer and Skook and purchased goods. This included Frank Stone and his family from Horneline Creek, Michel McCook and Jack Abou from City Cabins, and Charles and George Abou.

Christmas was a quiet day without any special celebrations. On December 28, Louis Boya and his family came up from Horneline Creek and went back the next day. On this trip, Louis purchased flour (11 kilograms), powdered milk, butter and coffee (450 grams each), and baking powder for a total of $8.35 and he added $2.00 of oats, for a total of $10.35.

The success of his business led Skook to continue his trading venture in 1946.

# 1946

### January 1–February 25 Diamond J Ranch

> *Feb 13* "I am leaving here February 27, 1946 for Fort St. James to take over the horses there as Rasmussen is raising hell."

Rasmussen had used horses provided by Skook when he was packing for surveyor Hugh Pattinson during the summer of 1944 and CM&S in 1945. Although Freer didn't provide specific details, it appears that Skook and Rasmussen had a disagreement about returning the horses.

### February 25–March 3 Trip to Fort Ware

> *Feb 27* "Met Jim and Fred McCook at Grizzly Creek. They are looking at the traps."

This is Freer's last diary entry referring to Jim McCook. McCook died of tuberculosis at Miller Bay Indian Hospital near Prince Rupert in April 1949. His death certificate indicated that he was a trapper, born in 1912, unmarried, and that he had had TB for at least two years. The Kwadacha at Fort Ware were part of the Stuart Lake Agency who sent their tuberculosis patients to the Miller Bay Hospital, so McCook died far from his home territory. Recently, there has been more focus on the health care Indigenous people received at the Indian hospitals. Carol Harrison, a nurse, has written a book titled *Miller Bay Indian Hospital*. The hospital operated from 1946 to 1971.

### March 3–13 Fort Ware

Freer commented in early March that there was widespread sickness at Fort Ware (likely from an influenza epidemic), and that several people were expected to die.

> *Mar 9* "Art van Somers and Del Miller came up from down river. Ludwig Smaaslet came down from Bower Creek. Everybody up river is terribly sick in bed. Everybody sick here."

### March 13–26 Fort Ware to Fort St. James

> *Mar 19* "Johnny Rasmussen and I went up to the police

station and talked things over. Johnny has agreed to everything Skook asked for."

*Mar 20* "I caught a ride out to Pinchi Lake with Jim Smith, a truck driver. I stayed with E. Bronlund. I will have work for the horses out here with the CMS Co. around Aiken Lake this year again."

Aiken Lake was in the Omineca district northwest of Manson Creek and Germansen Landing. Freer returned to Fort St. James on March 21.

*Mar 26* "Everything is fixed up now."

*March 27–April 15 Fort St. James, working with Hendry Kinniburgh*

*April 15–May 14 Southern BC, northern Washington, visiting family*

*May 14–28 Fort St. James, preparing for summer work*

*May 28–September 4 Omineca district*

Freer departed from Fort St. James for employment with Emil Bronlund, CM&S. This summer, Freer's work for CM&S involved considerable travel, transporting food, supplies and people to various CM&S camps through the Omineca district, all the way up to Thutade Lake again. Stuart Hoy, Fort St. James, was with Freer for part of the summer.

*June 28* "Stuart Hoy and I came down to Uslika Lake. Boss Bronlund and Roy Fraser arrived at 8:10 AM from Pinchi Lake."

*June 30* "E. Bronlund and Roy Fraser left Uslika Lake at 40½ mile and went up to the Ruby camp."

*July 12* "I sent 5 horses and a colt to the Thutade Lake camp for the rest of the season." Freer was at Thutade Lake from July 10 to July 14.

*July 31* "Came down to Uslika Lake to take Jerry Mason up Duck Creek.... Jerry Mason and his partner are at Uslika Lake and so is Emil Bronlund."

During the first half of August, Freer finally had some time without travelling and spent eleven days working at Ruby camp. On August 22, most of the men left, and Ruby camp closed the next day. Bush pilot Russ Baker flew in on August 25 and took out the remaining men. On September 4,

Freer and Ogilvie arrived at Uslika Lake, marking the end of the field season.

*September 9–October 25 Return trip to Diamond J Ranch*

> *Sept 9* "I left Uslika Lake with four horses packed on my way to Thutade Lake. Some stuff for Thutade, but most of loads are my rigging."

> *Sept 19* "I left my camp on the east side of Thutade Lake for the CMS camp on the west side. I went down from Thutade Lake and forded the Finlay River ½ mile below. I arrived in camp at 10 a.m. Snowing all day."

> *Sept 21* "I left here and found the horses up the lake about 12 miles. I brought them in. One of Russ Baker's planes was in and brought some supplies and Ray Fraser came in too. E. Bronlund, Roy Fraser and Doug Heavenor are staying down at the cabin on Thutade Lake." These were the horses that Freer had left at the lake on July 12.

> *Sept 23* "I left here at 8:30 AM with five head of horses. Forded the Finlay River at the outlet of Thutade Lake and picked up E. Bronlund, Roy Fraser and Doug Heavenor and am taking them on a prospecting trip down the Finlay River."

> *Sept 29* "I left the Thutade Lake Camp at 8 AM and arrived at E. Bronlund's camp at 4:15 PM down the Finlay River. The trail is very wet."

Freer left Thutade Lake on October 2. He arrived at Fort Ware on October 9 and spent the week there relaxing and visiting people before departing on October 16.

> *Oct 25* "I had a very good horse wrangle and left Gataga River at 8 AM. I met Craig Forfar about half way. Well, thank heavens this is another season finished. Arrived home at 2 PM…. Total time from Uslika Lake to Muddy River 152 hours."

Freer spent the last week of October working around the ranch. In his diary, Freer recorded visits from several Indigenous people. Most of them were purchasing supplies for the start of the trapping season. Skook's ledger journal listed their acquisitions.

*Dec 7* "Skook and Craig Forfar put up a tent across the creek for the Indians." Several Indigenous people came to the ranch during the following days.

*Dec 25* "This is another Xmas day passed, was in the kitchen all day. We had 3 chickens for Christmas dinner. Nobody did much outside of the chores. Stormy all day with north wind."

Frank George, a well-known Kaska hunting guide, came down from Frog River on the last day of 1946 and stayed overnight at the tent.

# 1947

*January 1–May 27 Diamond J Ranch*

In January, the men went out to check on the location of the horses almost daily. Several Indigenous people came to the Diamond J Ranch to acquire food and supplies.

*Jan 1* "Frank George bought some grub and returned to Frog River."

*Jan 2* "Joe McCook came down from City Cabins and bought some grub. He had a red fox and a fisher."

*Jan 3* "Joe McCook left for City Cabins with 175 lbs of grub."

*Jan 6* "Jack Abou, Frank Abou and George Abou came down from Frog River. They brought down some good fur. They got some grub and returned to Frog River."

*Jan 16* "Amos Alec came with his daughter. They are after supplies."

*Jan 17* "Amos Alec laid over. Skook got 3 skins from him. He bought some supplies. Amos Massetoe, Frank George and George Abou came down from Frog River. George Abou and Amos Massetoe returned."

*Jan 18* "Amos Alec and Frank George left for their respective lines."

Skook purchased a sewing machine and Freer was the main person to use it.

*Jan 14* "I did the cooking as usual and sewed on some new cinches that I am making."

"Crossing the Rancheria River ford on trail to Station N2." Freer on horse.
Land Title and Survey Authority of BC (LTSA)

From January 28 to February 3, the temperature dropped below –40°C every night. Skook went to the meadow and fed the mares and colts daily. Throughout February, the men continued to spend much of their time checking the horses and moving them to places where there was sufficient feed. Frank Cooke shot a large moose, and the men hauled loads of meat back to the ranch.

Between late February and mid-March, several people came to Skook's ranch to sell fur and purchase supplies. The last days of March were spent clearing brush, then piling and burning it. This removed some of the fire hazard in the area around the ranch and produced more grass for the horses and wildlife. Spring fire burning was an important part of the Indigenous ecology of the Kechika valley, and Skook incorporated it into the operation of the ranch.

From the end of March through April, there was a final flurry of activity related to spring trapping.

### May 27–June 17 Travel to the British Columbia-Yukon Boundary Survey and preparations for work

Skook finally had his first guide trip booked for the late summer of 1947. Frank Cooke arranged a thirty-day trip in the Kechika area with Rudy Pop and George C. Reifel, a wealthy Vancouverite. This was also the year that the BC government started registering guide areas, and Cooke recalled that Inspector Walter Gill, head of the Game Department office in Prince George, came to the Diamond J Ranch to visit Skook. Since no one else asked for a guiding area in the Kechika, Skook was able to get a large territory. Since Skook and Cooke were busy preparing for the hunting trip, Freer took charge of packing for the BC-Yukon boundary survey while Forfar handled an army survey.

> *May 27* "Fred Forsberg, Annie and I left the home place by boat and made Fish Creek. Jack Abou and family and Frank George came down with the boat. We picked up Jack George at Dust Cabin."

On May 28, they reached the camp at Mile 66, where the trail crosses the Kechika River. Skook arrived with the pack train the next afternoon and swam the horses across the river without any difficulty. Two days later, Skook, Cooke and Forfar left with the horses following the trail to Lower Post, while Freer and the Forsbergs travelled down the Kechika by boat. It took time to get everything organized at Lower Post. A government truck took Freer's rigging and equipment up the Alaska Highway.

In 1945, the BC-Yukon boundary survey resumed on the west side of Teslin Lake where the last station had been surveyed in 1908. From there it followed the 60th parallel east. The Alaska Highway crossed the 60th parallel in this area. In 1946, the survey moved east to the Watson Lake area where the Alaska Highway was close to the boundary again. Veteran BC land surveyor A.J. Campbell (BCLS #101) oversaw the project. (Campbell had been an assistant to A.O. Wheeler for the entire Alberta-BC boundary survey from 1913 to 1924.)

In 1947, Campbell began surveying the gap between the last station surveyed in 1945 and the first station in 1946. He had fifteen people working on his survey crew. There were two trucks and twenty-two pack horses. Michel McCook and Gerald Edzerza from Whitehorse were Freer's assistants. Chris Widrig states that Gerald Edzerza was one of the pioneer outfitters near Atlin, BC.

On June 11, Freer arrived at the main camp. Because there were so many men working on the boundary survey, it was necessary to maintain a sizeable supply of food. Fortunately, the Alaska Highway was only a few hours away on horseback. Freer went to the Alaska Highway several times during the summer, usually accompanied by Campbell, who would drive one of the government trucks to the nearest community where he could purchase supplies.

*June 18–October 11 Head packer for the British Columbia-Yukon Boundary Survey*

> *June 18* Freer and Edzerza "moved all the men and their dunnage out to the new camp on the Yukon and BC boundary line. We returned to Swift River Camp. A.J. Campbell is still here at Swift River."

> *June 19* "Packed up 12 loads and came up to the main camp. A.J. Campbell came up with us." In June, Freer made two more trips to the Alaska Highway.

During the first week of July, Freer and Edzerza blazed and cut trail and moved camp as the surveying progressed.

> *July 13* "Took 3 horses to the Swift River maintenance camp and brought back two loads of supplies and the mail." There were two more trips for supplies near the end of the month.

Work proceeded smoothly during August. The survey crews delineated the 60th parallel, while Freer and Edzerza located and moved camp every few days. Occasionally the men would go to the Alaska Highway to pick up supplies and mail.

*Aug 25* Freer and Tom Allen "took the horses to 707 on the highway. We met Gerald Edzerza and A.J. Campbell who came from Lower Post with supplies. We returned with 8 horse loads, arrived here at 5 PM." Freer moved camp once more on August 29.

Freer spent September 5 to 8 with Campbell, picking up and distributing supplies for Campbell and his assistant, Art Pollard, who had his own crew and camp.

Freer and Edzerza located their final camp of the season on September 17 and began cutting a trail to it. By September 20, they had reached the camp, and the men cut a trail to the Alaska Highway.

*Sept 21* "Fred Carlick and Gerald Edzerza moved the rest of the camp. I took 3 loads of freight to the highway." Freer returned to camp the next day.

*Sept 25* "Gerald Edzerza and I went ahead and located a camp for next year 1948. We sure picked a good one. We located trail too. All the crew are on line. They are even with camp." Two days later, Campbell finished the surveying for the 1947 season.

*Sept 29* The men started for the Alaska Highway. "I am taking the camp out. I have 15 loads." They arrived at the Alaska Highway at the Rancheria River by noon the next day.

Freer, assisted by Fred Carlick and Gerald Edzerza, began taking the horses to Lower Post on October 1.

*Oct 3* Freer's crew "stopped at 652 mile post at a deserted construction camp.... We were all paid off today. The wages go on until October 12, 1947. A.J. Campbell says I was the best man that he ever had."

*Oct 4* "We camped at the Watson Lake turn off and at a maintenance camp at mile 635. I met Skook at the beer parlour, also Mrs. Molly Forfar from Fort St. James. We certainly celebrated here."

*Oct 5* Freer and his crew arrived at Lower Post. "Skook met me again today at the BC and Yukon boundary line with some beer. Well I am off of the Alaska Highway for another year thank goodness. We celebrated some more as I had some rum here that I had ordered."

### October 11–21 Return trip to Diamond J Ranch

Freer left on October 11 with seven horses packed, and he caught up to Skook at 17 Mile the next day.

> *Oct 16* "Bill Thompson, a prospector, arrived from our place on way to Lower Post and on to Vancouver. He says the home place has been broken into."

> *Oct 17* The men reached the Kechika River. "The boys put all the supplies and rigging across the river ready for a swim. We are leaving the horses tied up for the night." Crossing the Kechika went smoothly on October 18.

On the return trip to the Diamond J, Freer "staked a section of land at Horn Creek. I will be staying there with a bunch of horses next winter." Freer was planning to have his own cabin farther north along the Kechika River.

Willard Freer, 1948. Hunter, guide, trapper. Willard Freer Family collection

### October 21–December 31 Diamond J Ranch

The men arrived at the Diamond J on October 21 where they found that a large amount of supplies had been taken and the house was dirty. Skook brought supplies back, and on October 26, several Indigenous people came to purchase goods, including Felix Johnnie. Most of them camped nearby and returned for more supplies the next day. From the last day of October through the first week of November, several people stopped at the Diamond J. Ranch.

In mid-November, wolves came into the area, and Freer noted their presence in several diary entries. Skook put out some poison in the Moose Licks.

*Nov 26* Freer's diary entry recorded an unintended consequence of using poison. "Skook's pet dog got a shot of poison, just about lost him."

*Dec 8* "I got 3 wolves at the mouth of Skook Creek."

In early December, some of the Indigenous inhabitants brought furs and purchased supplies. On December 6, the men put up the tent again. Throughout the month, the trappers in the area steadily brought in fur to exchange for supplies. Several trappers arrived between December 22 and 24, bringing a large quantity of fur.

> *Dec 25* Christmas was a quiet day. "Nobody did anything, was busy all day cooking. Jack George and Vincent Johnnie were over after a few groceries."

The last week of 1947 was quiet, with only a few trappers bringing in furs for barter.

# 1948

*January 1–May 27 Diamond J Ranch*

The first visitor to the ranch was Jack Abou on January 2 and again the following day.

> *Jan 5* "Joe McCook came down. He is courting Jack Abou's eldest daughter, he has stayed there steady all winter."

This winter marked the beginning of more frequent air transportation coming into the Kechika valley, making it easier to access supplies and travel.

> *Jan 8* "Craig Forfar and I went up river to mark a landing and meet the plane that comes in on January 10."

> *Jan 10* "The plane arrived at 10:30 AM from Lower Post with the mail and some supplies and returned to Lower Post. Craig Forfar and I returned home with the mail and supplies."

Famous bush pilot George Dalziel, who founded BC-Yukon Air Service, flew most of the planes into the Kechika valley that winter.

The arrival of the airplane found a quick response among the inhabitants. During the following three days, several Indigenous trappers brought fur and purchased goods. Throughout the rest of January, there was a steady exchange of fur and supplies at the ranch. Skook's ledger journal continued itemizing the goods purchased through the spring of 1948, while Freer's diaries documented the visits of the Indigenous people.

> *Jan 30* Dalziel flew to the valley. "He landed the supplies up at Denetiah Creek and landed again here. I went up river to get the stuff and Jack George and Felix Johnnie went up too."

In 1948 the famous Yukon bush pilot, George Dalziel, began to be noted in Freer's diary flying into the Kechika River valley. 98_30_26, Yukon Archives

Chris Widrig thought that Felix Johnnie was one of Robin Dalziel's top guides. He and his best friend, Doug Reid, died in 1976. The *Whitehorse Daily Star* printed an article on January 12, 1976, titled "No Inquest Planned Into Freezing Deaths," stating that "No inquest is expected to be called into the deaths of two Watson Lake men who were found frozen outside a cabin on the Cassiar-Stewart Road last Thursday. RCMP said the men are believed to have frozen to death with alcohol a contributing factor. Dead are Doug Reed and Felix Johnny, both in their late 40s."

*Jan 31* Several Indigenous people came for supplies. "Skook bought seven marten and one lynx." More trading occurred during the latter part of February and continued in early March. "Jack George was over with a lynx and a silver fox. I bought them, he took a few supplies."

*Mar 8* George Dalziel returned. "The plane came in from Dease Lake with our mail from Lower Post. He returned to Lower Post to bring a load of supplies for us tomorrow. I left here at 7 PM, went to Davie Creek to get Skook. We arrived home around midnight.... Skook and I wrote letters all night."

*Mar 9* "The plane arrived here at noon. He brought in supplies and took out our fur." Freer's diary entries recorded considerable trading activity in mid-March.

*Mar 27* Forfar "brought Ann [Forsberg] home as she has a sore jaw."

*Mar 29* "Skook fixed up Ann's jaw. He figures it is broken."
The following day Freer wrote that "Skook doctored Ann's jaw," and on March 31 there was a similar entry.

Dalziel flew into the valley with a load of food and the mail on April 7. He reported that the price of fur had dropped 25 per cent. Nevertheless, Skook and Freer continued buying fur and selling supplies during April. Freer's diary has several entries mentioning Indigenous people trapping beaver through the first half of May.

Preparations needed to be made for the trip to Lower Post.

*May 25* "Michel McCook and Frank George swamped in the Gataga River. They lost everything but Frank George saved his beaver. Dalziel came in at 7 PM with a load of supplies and returned to Lower Post."

### *May 27–June 6 Trip to Lower Post and preparation for work*

Freer left Diamond J Ranch on May 27. On June 5, the outfit arrived at the Dease River, which was at a low water level. Freer described crossing the Liard River the next day.

*June 6* "Bob Wilson and I crossed all the horses 4 at a time and all the horses came across very nice. I had 2 kids on the Dease River side leading horses to the boat and 2 more at McNab point taking them all away from the boat. We finished the crossing of everything just at dark. I stayed with the A.J. Campbell party tonight. This is the party I am to pack for with 18 head of horses on the BC Yukon boundary survey."

### *June 7–October 1 Head packer for the British Columbia-Yukon Boundary Survey*

On June 7, Freer took his outfit to the Y, the Alaska Highway turnoff to Watson Lake. Freer, Don Edzerza, his assistant, and the horses travelled west along the Alaska Highway, arriving at Big Creek, Mile 674, at 5:00 a.m. on June 12. Chris Widrig recalls that Don Edzerza was from Telegraph Creek and a Tahltan. He always wore a nice cowboy hat.

From Mile 674, Freer had to locate and cut a trail up Big Creek to the boundary line. Campbell's instructions were to continue surveying the boundary eastward from his last station in 1947. He had a large crew, with over half of the sixteen men returnees from the previous season. A.J. Campbell's party arrived on June 24, and they set up camp. On July 7, the crew moved to the campsite Freer had located the previous fall at the end of the season.

*July 8* "Don Edzerza and I went up to a cache we left last fall. We took up 4 head of horses. A bear had thrown everything off of the cache. Some of the stuff was spoiled."

On July 19, Freer and Don Edzerza took sixteen head of horses to the highway to pack in supplies that Campbell had purchased at Swift River and Lower Post. Freer accompanied Campbell on the trip to Lower Post and they stayed overnight at the hotel there.

The boundary survey commission's report describes an illness that affected Campbell's survey crew. "During August, Campbell's diary continually mentions a coughing epidemic which affected all members of the crew. The Indian members, in particular, were unable to shake off the illness. The settlements at Lower Post and Watson Lake were both quarantined by the malady which was finally diagnosed as whooping cough." On September 6, Campbell wrote:

With our weakened crew it was difficult to get much line cut. At one time I seriously considered closing the work and pulling out. But we hung on hoping for improvement from day to day and it finally came. We have christened our camps accordingly according to the situation. Our first from N4, Sanatorium, because it was thought it sounded like one. Next Hospital camp—we put some of the worst to bed for a couple of days.... Then Improvement camp—as there was definite signs of improvement, and this one I think we can call Recovery as while there is considerable coughing it has lessened very much and the crew all seem to be feeling capable of a day's work.

*Aug 13* Freer wrote "Some of the men are out on line. There are 4 men sick in bed here [whooping cough—a note added later]. I had to help in the kitchen."

The next day Freer noted that four men were sick, but the rest were out on line. Freer's diary for August 20 and 21 mentions sickness among the crew again. One of the horses got sick and had to be shot.

The men moved to their last camp of the season on September 14.

*Sept 20* "The boys finished the line today at noon.... I washed coronas and packed equipment to go out tomorrow."

*Sept 21* "Don Edzerza and I had a very good wrangle and took 6 loads to the road [Alaska Highway]."

On September 22, they moved everything out to the Alaska Highway at Mile Post 652-½. Three days later, they left camp at Mile 652 and camped at the Y at Mile 635. A large truck came up and moved Campbell's camp to Lower Post on September 26.

### September 26–October 18 Return to Diamond J Ranch

> *Oct 4* Freer started back to the Diamond J Ranch. "I crossed 54 head of horses with Bob Wilson's boat. It took us 3 hours to cross the whole outfit. Donald McCook and Leo Johnnie stayed with the horses. 2 Indian boys were out and brought in 5 head of the missing horses." Freer noted that three Johnnie family boys were with him.

> *Oct 14* They reached the Kechika River crossing. "Everything went fine. Got all the equipment across the river at dark. We used two rafts." The men arrived at the ranch on October 18.

### October 18–December 31 Diamond J Ranch

At the beginning of November, "Craig Forfar and Michel McCook left for City Cabins with two pack horse loads of grub for Michel this winter."

> *Nov 8* "Jack Abou and Jack George were over and got a few supplies along with two windows." The next day Freer filled the cellar with vegetables. Several people came to the ranch during the latter part of the month.

From late November to December, there were several entries regarding a shortage of food.

> *Nov 29* "Charlie Boya came up from Fish Creek last night and returned to Fish Creek. They are starving down there."

> *Dec 10* "Charlie Boya and 2 of Charlie Porter's kids came up. They are all starving as they can't get any meat. Jack Abou and his daughter were over."

> *Dec 11* "The Porters were over and went back over to Jack Abou's. Charlie Boya went with them. We got a wire out to get supplies into the Indians that are starving at Fish Lake." The Department of Indian Affairs was responsible for providing food to any groups of Indigenous people who were starving.

*Dec 19* "Charlie, Louis Boya and his family came up from Fish Creek and are starving. The plane was in to Charlie Porter's at Fish Lake with supplies."

*Dec 25* "This is another Christmas gone. Craig Forfar went to the lake to look up 6 head of horses there. He found them. Jack Abou, Joe McCook and Louis Boya were over and borrowed a dog sled. Skook came home at 2:30 from Cottonwood Flats.... I did the usual outside chores and the housework and got a Christmas dinner ready."

*Dec 31* "Well, this is the end of another year. Has been a tough winter so far. I lost 2 horses on the survey last summer and one colt at Big Creek Mile 674 Alaska Highway. There were several died here during the summer and Two Bit's colt and 2 colts this winter so far.... Louis Boya and Jack Abou were over. Craig Forfar and I made an airplane landing at the boat landing."

In the government report he made at the end of 1948, Campbell noted Freer's involvement with the BC-Yukon boundary survey. "Willard Freer, packer for two years, had been packer for Mr. Ney in 1944, making it his third year in connection with the boundary."

# 1949

*January 1–April 21 Diamond J Ranch*

Freer was waiting for Dalziel to arrive with his airplane at the start of the year.

*Jan 1* "I cooked up a chicken dinner and did the outside chores along with the usual house work."

Dalziel finally arrived on the morning of January 7, and Jack Abou, Louis Boya and Joe McCook came over later in the day for supplies.

Dalziel was scheduled to arrive again on January 14, but he didn't appear until five days later, because cold weather (below −50°C) had prevented him from flying.

*Jan 19* "Skook and I both met the plane. All the Indians were there and they came up here and got some stuff and the clothes that they had ordered."

Dalziel came with Ron Sampson, the Indian agent from Telegraph Creek, on January 25. They stayed at the Diamond J overnight and returned to Lower Post the next day. Sampson likely came to check on the situation

Painting saddles, Coal River. Willard Freer Family collection

of the Indigenous people who lived around Fish Lake and had been reported to be starving.

> *Jan 29* "Louis and Charlie Boya went to Fish Creek to look after their traps. Louis's family went down too."

> *Jan 31* "We had a big turkey feed. Dalziel came in from Lower Post at noon and snowing like hell. Louis and Charlie Boya came up from Trail Creek at 7:30 PM."

> *Feb 1* "Dalziel was in at 10 AM with a load of grub for the Indians." This food probably was a result of Sampson's visit.

On February 4, Dalziel arrived with more supplies. The next day, three of Jack Abou's children came over to the ranch, and two days later two of Jack Abou's daughters came to buy a few items. Skook and Freer did more trading with the Indigenous people in February, and Freer recorded the activities.

> *Feb 26* "Received a wire from Victoria stating that there will be 20 head of horses on boundary survey this season with A.J. Campbell."

> *Apr 13* "Skook went along the pasture dividing fence and stumbled and cut the back of his head quite bad."

> *Apr 14* "Skook's axe cut bled quite a lot."

> *Apr 17* "I baked bread and was busy all day getting ready to go to Horn Creek to start to build." On Freer's birthday, April 19, he and Forfar left with 5 light loads.

> *Apr 23* Freer moved his camp "to the river where Louis Boya had a cabin which burnt down two years ago.... I am camped about a mile south of Horn Creek."

## April 23–May 19 Freer's cabin

Freer spent some time working around his cabin site before leaving for the summer.

## May 19–September 26 Prepare for surveying; head packer for the British Columbia-Yukon Boundary Survey

> *May 19* "Dalziel came in at 4 PM. He has his new plane, a Waco. I went to Lower Post with Dalziel to get things started for the season. I was 45 minutes coming out."

A.J. Campbell came up from his camp on May 27. At Lower Post there were several survey parties waiting to work, and Freer helped them get organized. Edgar Dopp, one of the Bedaux Expedition cowboys that Freer knew, also assisted.

The Boundary Commission report for 1949 stated that the objective for the field season was to complete the surveying and cutting of the 60th parallel from Teslin Lake to N6, the final astrofix that Ney had established in 1944. A decision was made to start the surveying at N6, the eastern end of the line.

> "The lines were run from east to west instead of what would appear as the natural way. It was decided to do this, with the approval of the Commissioners, for several reasons.... The main reason was that several miles of the west end of the line could be reached from the highway, and once the camp was back to it, the need for the pack train would be over. This appeared to be important, as it had been estimated that it would take until the end of October to finish the work; and the freeze-up with its attendant lack of feed and icy rivers to ford, might make it very difficult for the horses to reach their home range. It would also mean a considerable savings in cost of the survey."

> *June 20* "Took 14 loads of supplies and equipment ahead to N6 north of Crooked Lake.... Charlie Boya and Ernest Frank are my 2 assistants this year." The surveying began on June 23 at N6. Initially the work proceeded smoothly, but heavy rain at the end of the month slowed progress.

> *July 1* "The camp is flooded now.... A.J. Campbell is going to Dawson Creek tomorrow."

> *July 4* Freer moved the camp west to Loon Lake. During this move "the egg horse went over backwards and smashed the eggs all up."

> *July 9* Campbell returned from Dawson Creek with about 1,400 kilograms of supplies. "We fixed up the loads, 14 horse loads."

On July 18, Freer wrote that Charlie Boya was sick in bed. The next day there were two men sick in camp. The men moved camp on July 23, and the following day Freer wrote that he was sick.

*July 24* "There are 4 sick men in camp too. There seems to be a damn flu going around." On July 26, three men, including Freer, were still sick in camp.

Despite sickness, work continued on establishing the 60th parallel. The men spent a lot of time clearing and marking the 60th parallel, for the boundary line had to be 1.8 metres width at skyline. Freer made several references to monuments surveyed and established on the boundary line. The surveying proceeded smoothly. Freer moved camp several times. Because of the size of the crew, a large amount of supplies and equipment needed to be transported, so it took at least two trips to move camp.

On August 17, Campbell's crew reached a feature called the High Ridge and established camp nearby. The High Ridge was crucial to the successful completion of this section of the BC-Yukon boundary survey. It was almost completely visible along the line from the starting point at N6 west to R5, the Ross astrofix where the survey had finished in 1948. This ridge was also close to the 60th parallel. Most of the 60th parallel in this section could be connected to monuments along the High Ridge. The boundary commission report stated: "The important feature is that the High Ridge lay close to the line, thus giving assurance that the resulting bearing between R5 and N6 would be of sufficient accuracy. This was completely demonstrated in the results obtained. Also, the cairn on 'High North' proved very useful and comforting to check the position of the line from many points both east and west of it."

Campbell spent several days surveying on the High Ridge while the crew demarcated the 60th parallel through this area. The next move, on August 22, was to Coal River. By August 25, the crew had surveyed almost to the Coal River camp. The next afternoon Dalziel arrived with a load of food.

*Aug 26* "All the crew were out on the line today and crossed Coal River with the line at noon. They are making good time.... Dalziel got stuck on the bar here with his plane."

One of the crew, Phil Wattsoff, cut his foot badly on the last day of August. On September 3, Campbell decided that Phil needed to go to the hospital at Watson Lake, so a plane came and took the injured man out.

*Sept 5* "AJ Campbell and I went to Watson Lake Y and picked up Phil Wattsoff and took him to Watson Lake and sent him to Vancouver to get his foot looked after properly."

The men continued cutting trail and surveying the 60th parallel through September.

*Sept 26* "Moved the whole camp out to the Alaska Highway at mile 577.... Well I am finished and will start for Lower Post and Muddy River tomorrow."

## September 26–October 15 Return to the Diamond J

Freer reached Lower Post on September 29 and spent the next day getting ready to go back to the Kechika valley. "I will be taking in 35 head of horses."

*Oct 15* Freer returned to the Diamond J. "Skook was out but arrived back at 4 PM. Louis Boya and family came up from Fish Creek and went across the river where all the Indians are camped."

## October 15–25 Return trip to Freer's cabin

On October 24 Freer departed from Skook's with three horses loaded.

*Oct 25* "Went through to Horn Creek where I shall stay now." According to some people, Skook provided Freer with some horses when he moved to Horn Creek.

## October 25–December 31 Freer's cabin

On the last day of October, Freer started to skid in the logs and poles for a small 12 x 12 cabin. By November 3, he was finished. Freer continued working on his cabin throughout November. Freer finished putting the roof on and banked the building up by December 5.

*Dec 10* "Well, I finally got moved into the cabin and it is sure a lot pleasanter and warmer than the tent. Had my weekly bath, wrote a couple letters."

*Dec 14* Forfar and Charlie Boya arrived from the Diamond J Ranch headed for Lower Post for the holidays. "Joe and Louis Boya and family along with Jack George came down and are headed for Fish Creek. They are camped at Horn Creek. Joe Boya was over here."

*Dec 21* "I heard a plane at noon which landed on Scoop Lake with Jack George and a load of grub. Jack came here just at dark from Scoop Lake. He went on through to the Indian's camp at Skook's." The next day Freer went to Scoop Lake and picked up his radio and Skook's box of stuff.

*Dec 23* "Put up the radio and fixed up an aerial. The radio sure booms in. It is a new one, I paid $92 for it at Christy's."

Christmas was quiet and the temperature was −40°C. During the last week of the year the temperature was below −50°C every night.

The Boundary Commission report at the end of 1949 stated: "During the summer seasons 1945–49, demarcation of the 60th parallel had fulfilled the original purpose for which the British Columbia-Yukon-Northwest Territories boundary commission had been formed. Beginning at Teslin Lake the boundary had been extended eastward to Astrofix N6 at Smith River, approximately 40 miles east [64 kilometres] of the last crossing of the Alaska Highway."

The survey of the northern BC boundary along the 60th parallel halted after 1949 but resumed in 1952. The Boundary Commission report stated: "Exploration for and discovery of petroleum and natural gas was rapidly being extended northwestward from central Alberta.... It became imperative to extend the northern boundary of British Columbia to its eastern end."

# THE 1950S: 1950–1959

## HIGHLIGHTS

In the fall of 1949, Freer started construction of his own cabin on a parcel of land along the Kechika River about thirty kilometres north of Skook Davidson's Diamond J Ranch. Thereafter, he always considered this place as his home. Freer continued the trading store that he and Skook had started, and in 1951, he acquired his own trapline.

Every summer and fall during this decade, Freer had a packing job related to geology and mineral claims. He packed for CM&S again, and spent several summers with Northwestern Explorations, the BC branch of Kennco, a major mining company. He also had two field seasons with the Geological Survey of Canada.

## 1950 AND 1951

Freer's notebook with his 1950 and 1951 diaries is the only one that is missing between 1942 and 1975. Some of Skook Davidson's diary fragments cover parts of 1950 and 1951, and they indicate that Freer packed for a major mining exploration company in the summer of both years. All Freer's summer work during the 1950s was for mineral exploration or the federal Canadian Geological Survey.

Kennecott Copper, one of the largest mining companies in North America in the 1950s, had a Canadian subsidiary called Kennco. Northwestern Explorations, Kennco's western office, was based in Vancouver. In April 1951, Dave Barr began working for Northwestern Explorations as a junior geologist. He wrote a memoir titled *One Lucky Canuck* that includes descriptions of the projects the company did during the 1950s when Freer packed for them. Northwestern Explorations had a small permanent staff. In addition to Barr, geologists Gerry Noel and John Anderson worked for the company, along with a secretary. Paul Hammond, Northwestern Exploration's manager, lived and worked in Penticton.

Freer packed for this company from 1950 to 1954, and in 1956. From 1950 to 1953 he worked on Northwestern Explorations projects in the Omineca district northwest of Fort St. James. Another packer, Buster Groat, was with Freer in 1951. It appears that Freer spent the winters of 1949–50 and 1950–51 in the Kechika valley. Although he had his own place north of the Diamond J Ranch, Freer frequently got together with Skook. Skook still made the arrangements for summer employment until Freer began packing for the Geological Survey of Canada in 1958.

In 1951, Freer acquired Fred Forsberg's trapline, which mainly encompassed the Rabbit River and Netson Creek drainage that paralleled the Kechika to the east. Freer's cabin in the Kechika valley was near Horneline Creek at the start of the trail to Horneline Lake. This provided the easiest access between the Kechika and Rabbit drainages. Fred and Annie Forsberg moved to Lower Post in 1951 and are only mentioned in Freer's diary a few times after that. Freer and Groat returned from packing for Northwestern Explorations on October 20, 1951. On November 7, the two men went on a ten-day trip to Rabbit River. Around Christmas, both flew to Watson Lake. Freer then went to Fort St. James to visit friends and was there at the beginning of 1952.

The event with the most profound impact on residents of the Kechika River valley during 1950 and 1951 was the establishment of a residential school at Lower Post for Indigenous children who lived in northern BC and southern Yukon. The Catholic Church administered the school for the federal government and combined it with the day school that they had already established in the community. The school at Lower Post taught the elementary school curriculum.

Lower Post Residential School opened in the fall of 1951. In one of his diary fragments, Skook documented an incident in which he was involved.

> *Dec 4* "Dal [bush pilot George Dalziel] left word he wanted to see me. He is coming in for two of Jack Abou's kids who are going to school Lower Post. Waited all day but he did not show up."

> *Dec 21* "Dal's wife wired. Dal had a bad ankle. Willard and Buster very sad." They had planned to fly out for Christmas.

> *Dec 22* "Dal came in. Willard got out. Dal due in tomorrow to take out Buster."

> *Dec 23* "Dal did not come in."

> *Dec 24* "Dal came in, took out Jack Abou's kids. Will come in tomorrow for Buster."

The establishment of Lower Post Residential School had a profound impact on the lives of the Indigenous people of northern BC and southern Yukon. It affected the personal lives of the children and almost every family. Many experienced violence and alcoholism, and the effects of attending residential school remain for Indigenous people and communities.

# 1952

*January 1–March 18 Visiting family*

At the beginning of the year, Freer was at Fort St. James visiting people he knew, including Slim Powney, Alec Leggatt, and Doug Heavenor. He left on January 8 to visit family members in BC and Washington.

On January 30, Willard went to Penticton and met Paul Hammond from Northwestern Explorations.

> *Jan 31* "Went up to the Northwestern Exploration Limited and made arrangements for work for the following season."

In February, Freer went to Penticton and stayed with his brother Harold and his family whom he hadn't seen since 1931.

> *Feb 10* "Harold and I drove down to Chelan across the US border to Percy Freer who I haven't seen since he was a small kid."

Harold and Willard spent two days with their youngest brother. On March 11, Willard travelled to Fort St. John where he stayed with his brother Frank for a while. Then he left by bus for Lower Post and started working at Christy's Lodge on March 18.

*March 18–April 3 Christy's Lodge*

During the 1950s, Freer began to spend part of each year working at a lodge on the Alaska Highway. Initially he worked for Christy's at Lower Post, doing a variety of jobs, but mainly handling the gas pumps. He continued employment there after Bud Wright took a five-year lease on the lodge in 1955.

In the 1960s, Freer worked at the Fireside Inn, a lodge located near the junction of the Kechika and Liard Rivers east of Lower Post. Jack and Florence Christy also owned Fireside but sold it to Ken and Margo Windrem in the late 1950s. Watson Lake Flying Service flew regularly into the Kechika beginning in the late 1950s. Freer acquired a riverboat, and a boat trip up the Kechika to his cabin took one or two days, while downstream travel took less than a day. Freer still spent most of his time in the wilderness area of northern BC.

> *Mar 24* "Inspector Gill, game warden from Prince George, is flying here, dropping poison for wolves." In his diary entries for late March, Freer noted that there were "lots of Americans going through to Alaska," and that Christy's Lodge was very busy.

## April 4–May 20 Kechika River valley

On April 3, Freer went to the Watson Lake Hotel after supper so that he would be ready for an early flight.

> *Apr 4* "Well, I made it to the Muddy today. Had to land below Dust cabin as the river is all opened above. I walked up to Cottonwood Flats and met Skook. He was glad to see me."

> *Apr 6* "Went down to Davie Creek to see what happened to Skook.... Skook said he dropped from a blackout and laid in the snow for several hours." Fortunately, the weather was warm.

Freer left on April 16 for Horneline Lake to trap beaver. Ten days later, he brought his third and final load to Horneline Lake.

> *Apr 30* Freer left the lake and went "east over a low summit and hit the Rabbit River up from 4th cabin. Never found the cabin. Rabbit River is still frozen solid, not much snow in the valley."

> *May 2* "I left my camp at daylight and arrived at the new cabin at 10 AM. The dog and I both have damn heavy packs, are sure tired. Lots of ice in Rabbit River, no chance to trap beaver. Saw four caribou and one lynx."

After spending a few days exploring the area, Freer arrived back at the new cabin on May 5. During the return trip he sprung all the traps, catching one beaver. On May 12, on his way to the Diamond J, Freer met Skook at Cottonwood Flats checking the horses.

## May 20–June 18 Travel to Omineca district

Freer and Henry Charlie left the Diamond J on May 20. Frank George, Don McCook and Charlie came to help Willard cross the Gataga River. Freer wrote that "Henry Charlie is going to Fort Ware with me." On May 27, the two men arrived at Fort Ware.

> *May 30* "Swam the horses at the mouth of the White [Kwadacha] River and came up to the south side of the Finlay River. Roy Pettie, HBC manager, couldn't start his kicker, so Francis Charlie and John Poole helped to cross in HBC boat. I paid them $5."

Freer reached the Thutade Lake camp on June 4. He resumed his journey to Germansen Landing on June 7, basically following the same route that he had used when packing for Bronlund in 1946. On June 12, Freer arrived at the camp at 69 Mile on the Mesilinka River. He couldn't ford the river at the crossing because the current was too swift, so he used the cable car to transport goods and equipment and swam the horses. He crossed the Osilinka at a very deep ford on June 14. Two days later he camped at Nina Creek on the Germansen road.

> *June 17* "Met a bulldozer crew pushing a road through to the Osilinka River. They are stuck in a mudhole…. The government's building a bridge over the Omineca River."

*June 19–August 22 Packer for Northwestern Explorations in Omineca district*

> *June 19* "Dave Barr came in from the Nina Lake Prospect and Paul Hammond drove in from Penticton."

In *One Lucky Canuck,* Barr wrote:

> In 1952 I had my first experience with the use of packhorses for prospecting and geological parties largely dependent on these beasts of burden for most of their day-to-day transportation needs. The packers I was to meet and rely on prior to the transition to helicopter travel several years later were all true frontiersmen. Comfortable with the outdoors, self-reliant, they were at ease with themselves. They were to include Buster Groat, Cariboo John Bendicksen, Albert Alexander, Willard Freer and the legendary Skook Davidson. My time with them was far too brief.

Barr described Freer as "a lean cowboy who never seemed to change appearance, because he was almost perpetually garbed in leather chaps and a weather-beaten, sweat-stained ten gallon hat. He worked for many years for Skook Davidson who maintained a well-established corral of pack and saddle horses for exploration crews and hunters at his base in the Kechika River area."

On June 20, Freer took Barr and Hammond out to the Nina Lake prospect and brought them back to Germansen Landing two days later. The bulldozer was still stuck. During the return trip, Freer met Tommy Walker, the well-known outfitter who had a lodge on the Spatsizi Plateau. "T.A. Walker is in with 18 head of horses headed for Cold Fish Lake."

From the last week of June to early August, Freer made trips to Germansen almost weekly. He noted progress on construction of the bridge over the Omineca River. Dave Barr arrived from Fort St. James by vehicle late in the evening of July 25 and stayed for a while.

*Aug 6* "Went to Germansen landing. Took Dave Barr in and he left for Fort St. James with his company car. The Atlas Construction Company have the bridge piling across the river."

## August 22–29 Travel to Mooseskin Johnny Lake

There was a sudden change to Freer's fieldwork.

*Aug 22* "Paul Hammond wants me urgently to go to Mooseskin Johnny Lake via Telkwa to pack in a drill and gas to the Grizzly claims. Apparently the packer there can't do the job.... Slim Powney and I left Germansen Landing and arrived in Fort St. James early. Had a good trip and saw Dave Barr."

The next day, Freer and Barr went to Vanderhoof to Clarence Reierson's place to pick up six horses to take to Telkwa. On August 25, Willard travelled to Telkwa with Nels Irving, and they unloaded the horses at a coal mine twelve kilometres west of Telkwa. Freer stayed at the community that night and went to a picture show.

## August 29–September 22 Packer for Northwestern Explorations at Mooseskin Johnny Lake

On August 29, Freer travelled to a campsite about three kilometres east of Mooseskin Johnny Lake. The next day he went to the Grizzly Claims camp at the timberline above the lake. During the following days, Freer transported gas and other items up to the claim. Each round-trip took about ten hours.

*Sept 11* Jim Scott, from Kennco's office in Vancouver, arrived. "Well, looks as though everything is all off and there won't be any drilling. I packed 64 cases of gas to the Grizzly Claims drill site."

*Sept 12* "Left here at daylight with a note to Paul Hammond in Telkwa to stop the drill from coming in."

*Sept 13* "Took Jim Scott from Vancouver office, Dave Simpson, geologist, from Edmonton and Bill Jones from Victoria down to Mooseskin Johnny Lake to go out. I returned to the Grizzly Claims camp. The plane came in at 3:15 PM and cleaned out everything at the lake including these men in trips."

*Sept 14* "Well, I am starting to move the camp out as the drilling part is all off."

On September 15, Freer went up to the camp and brought down all the crew and five heavy loads of equipment and personal dunnage. Freer travelled to Telkwa with five heavy loads on September 21. The next day Johnny Lindsay took Freer and the horses back to Clarence Reierson's ranch.

*Sept 22* "Lindsay stopped in all the beer parlors. He sure drove fast."

*September 22–October 27 End of summer activities and travel to Christy's Lodge*

Don Stoker took four of Freer's horses to the Erhorn Ranch west of Vanderhoof to winter. Then Freer travelled to Fort St. James and spent almost a month putting away equipment at the Kennco warehouse at the police station. He spent several evenings visiting friends.

On October 24, he travelled to Prince George, and from there flew to Watson Lake on October 25.

*October 27–December 31 Christy's Lodge*

*Oct 27* Freer began working at Christy's Lodge. "There was a Halloween dance in masquerade at Watson Lake Y. Jim Iseman stole Christy's taxi car and smashed it up."

During November and December, Freer recorded a variety of tasks that he did at Christy's Lodge.

*Dec 25* "Jack Christy, Jerry Jensen and I went to Iron Creek and pulled the trailer up to the top of the hill and returned."

*Dec 31* "Jack Christy returned from Whitehorse with the gas and quite a few went to Watson Lake airport to the New Year dance.... There was a dance at Lash Collison's which was well attended."

# 1953

*January 1–February 28 Christy's Lodge*

*Jan 1* "Nobody did anything much today but the odds and ends around Christy's and I went visiting in the evening."

On January 8, the weather turned cold, going below −40°C for a few days, and the garage became busy with cars needing to be repaired or have their fuel lines thawed out. On January 11, the temperature went below –50°C.

> *Jan 12* "There were plenty of vehicles around all day. Very cold, lots of outfits froze up. The upper Liard and Watson Lake gas pumps were froze up and the cars came here after gas and returned." It started to warm up on January 14, and there were more cars travelling on the highway again.

In his diary entry for February 6, Freer noted that he was working at the store every night from 6:00 p.m. to 12:00 p.m. When Joe Landry came in to Lower Post, Freer would help him unload the fuel.

> *Feb 7* "Joe Landry and I unloaded all the fuel. Filled up the power plant and put about 200 gallons in the hotel. Joe left for Dawson Creek. I took more ice off the hotel room."

> *Feb 28* "Went to Horn Lake by Dalziel in the Waco aircraft." There was only about 15 centimetres of snow at the lake.

## February 28–April 8 Kechika River valley

On March 2, Freer packed all of Skook's grub that Dalziel had left there off the river and put it in the cache. The next afternoon, Freer arrived at the Diamond J. Skook was glad to see him and the two men spent several days visiting and doing chores around the ranch. On March 10, they started going out every day to check the horses.

Freer remained at the Diamond J ranch until March 23. Then he did a variety of work for a few weeks.

> *Apr 7* Dalziel arrived as expected and Freer went back to Watson Lake with him. "Flo Christy sent a car up for me." He resumed working at Christy's the next day.

## April 8–April 29 Christy's Lodge

> *Apr 19* "Joe Landry came in from Dawson Creek with a part load of diesel. The power plant is on the bum and will have to be shut down for a major overhaul."

> *Apr 20* "This was a mad house all day. The Lister light plant was started and the large power plant was shut down. The hotel was filled and people sleeping in the lobby. Trucks stalled here for tire repair, 3 cars broke down and sure lots of activity around."

*April 29–May 13 Travel to Fort St. James and visit with friends*

On April 29, Freer left with Joe Landry on his trip to Dawson Creek for fuel, the first part of the trip to Fort St. James for packing with Kennco in the summer. When they arrived at Fort St. John, Freer went to stay with his brother Frank.

> *May 6* "Took the plane to Prince George. I left Fort St. John and there were 5 planes on the airport [at] once."

*May 14–September 29 Packer for Northwestern Explorations*

Freer went to Fort St. James the next day and stayed with friends. On May 14, Dave Barr, Jack Greenaway, and Jack Anderson of Kennco arrived from Vancouver. Barr described the company's activities.

> In 1953 we used pack horses throughout the summer during a four-month program in the Nina Lake area.... I was the party-chief of a program designed to explore the lead-zinc-silver potential of a limestone belt traced for 50 kilometres northerly between the Omineca and Osilinka rivers. An average of 16 men were employed from late May to September in several capacities including geological assistant, prospectors, labourer, cook and a packer. Initial supplies and equipment were trucked from Fort St. James, about 200 kilometres north to Germansen Landing. These were shuttled by float-plane to Nina Lake and from there by a pack train of nine horses to a base camp. During the season seven additional fly camps were established at points along the limestone belt in the course of trail cutting and geological mapping.
>
> The horses packed in our total requirements. The heaviest load I can recall seeing loaded and packed was a rock drill weighing almost 200 pounds [90 kilograms], which had to be balanced off with a load of equivalent weight. This was packed by our lead horse, a large gray mare, the undisputed leader of the group....
>
> The pack horses made weekly trips between Germansen Landing and base camp to obtain fresh supplies, transport mail and out-going samples for assay. Again, we had no reliable radio communication; however, Germansen Landing did, and it could be reached in a day's travel.

# DR. HARRY VERNEY WARREN (1904–1998)

Dr. Warren was a famous BC geologist and professor at UBC for forty years, along with being a person of many talents. After receiving a BA in 1926 and a BSc in geological engineering in 1927 from UBC, he went to Oxford as a Rhodes Scholar. Warren was selected for Canada's track team for the 1928 Olympics in Amsterdam, and the following year he completed his doctorate at Oxford.

In 1932, Warren began teaching at UBC, initially as a lecturer, then a professor, and later an emeritus professor. Concurrently, he worked on projects related to the mining industry, and a couple of them were with Kennco. He is considered to be one of the pioneers in biogeochemistry, using interdisciplinary studies from biology, chemistry and geology to develop new techniques in the discovery of minerals.

Warren was associated with the BC and Yukon Chamber of Mines for many years, and was elected a member of the Canadian Mining Hall of Fame. The award stated:

> A lateral thinker long before the term was coined, Harry Warren applied his intellectual curiosity and scientific mind to the field of geochemistry, where he made remarkable contributions to prospecting and mineral exploration. He was a pioneer in a discipline which came into its own, to a large extent, through his efforts. In his special area of research—bio-geochemistry, of which he is acknowledged as the founding father—he studied the metal content of plants and vegetation as a guide to buried mineral deposits. From his findings, he went on to propose the now-recognized connection between trace elements and the environment and health.

Warren received the Order of Canada for his "contribution to science, particularly the development of new techniques in the discovery of minerals." He also received the Order of British Columbia which stated: "Dr. Harry Warren might well be described as a 20th century Renaissance man—athlete, Rhodes Scholar, sportsman, scientist, researcher and teacher. He was renowned in all of them."

Warren was active in sports associations and was the founding president of the Canadian Field Hockey Association. He was elected to the BC Sports Hall of Fame.

On May 15, Freer went to the Erhorn Ranch to pick up the horses that he had left there for the winter. Two days later, Freer and his nine head of horses arrived at Fort St. James in the evening. He spent two days getting organized for the trip.

> *May 20* "I made a four hour trip to the top of Pope Mountain for the Forestry and made $20."

> *May 21* Freer left Fort St. James with the horses, bound for Germansen Landing. "Dave Barr and Jack Greenaway took hay and oats for me to the Nation River. Blackburn's Northern Freighters will leave tomorrow with loads."

On May 26, Freer arrived at Germansen Landing by mid-afternoon. Dave Barr, Paul Hammond, and other crew members came in by truck.

> *May 27* "Went to Nina Creek where the Atlas construction outfit are camped. They are putting a road through the north towards Aiken Lake."

The next day, Freer set up camp at the east end of Nina Lake waiting for a plane to bring in seven tons of supplies from Germansen Lake. The plane came in on May 29, bringing men and supplies in several trips. The day after, Freer started packing the loads to the camp at Meadow Lake. By June 6, Freer had packed fifty-six loads of material and supplies to the camp.

On June 7, Freer went to Germansen Landing late in the evening to meet Paul Hammond. The next day, Freer took him to Camp Lake, the main camp. During the following week, the crew set up camp and cut trail. In the latter part of June, Freer was busy shoeing some horses and moving supplies and the camp. Freer also made a couple of trips to Germansen Landing. On June 30, Willard "moved Dave Barr's camp north to the summit."

Freer continued to move supplies and equipment as needed during the first half of July. On July 16 and 17, he went with Dave Barr and some senior executives to visit a couple of the locations where the men were working.

> *July 21* "George Ordway, Jim Scott and Dave Barr were out looking things over. Sure found some good mineral."

The next day, Freer took Jim Scott and George Ordway to the road where they picked up a truck and went to Fort St. James, departing for Vancouver the next day. Freer continued to move men and equipment during the last week of July.

Freer went to Germansen Landing to pick up Paul Hammond when he arrived on August 9. He took him to a few camps, then brought Hammond out to Germansen Landing on August 21. Freer waited there for Dr. Harry

Warren's arrival on August 22 and brought him to the main camp the next day. Freer was busy during September moving people and packing supplies, and he made several trips to Germansen Landing.

> *Aug 24* "I took Dave Barr and Dr. Warren up to No. 2 camp on the summit north of main camp." Two days later Freer brought them back to the main camp, and he returned Dr. Warren to Germansen Landing on August 28.

> *Sept 26* "Alex Mitchell and I loaded seven head of horses and arrived in Fort St. James at 8:30 PM. I turned the horses loose in Lawrence Dickinson's yard."

> *Sept 29* "Alex Mitchell and I loaded the 3 horses and loaded the back of the truck with the camping equipment and part of my outfit. We arrived in Fort St. James around 8 PM.... We unloaded all the equipment in the warehouse at the police station and I unloaded the horses at Lawrence Dickinson's corral." The next day the horses were taken to Erhorn's Ranch west of Vanderhoof for the winter.

## September 29–October 28 Work at Fort St. James

Freer spent most of October working at Kennco's warehouse in Fort St. James.

## October 29–November 13 Travel to Lower Post

On October 29, Freer went to Vanderhoof, the beginning of his return trip to Lower Post.

> *Nov 2* "I left Prince George by Northern stages for Dawson Creek, fare $10.20. There were 3 women and I on the bus. We collided with a car with 5 occupants on way to Vancouver 125 miles west of Dawson Creek. No passengers in the bus were hurt but my teeth were broken in the collision. In the car one woman's leg broke in 2 places, one woman seriously hurt in chest, arms and ribs, one man minor cuts, 2 children minor cuts. We were brought into Dawson Creek by cars that were travelling. The bus driver had to stay with the accident. The car was smashed very badly. Snowing and very slippery. Snow plows out. I stayed at the Palace Hotel and never again."

Freer remained in Dawson Creek until his dental repairs were finished. On November 13, he flew to Watson Lake on a Canadian Pacific flight. Flo

Christy picked him up at the airport, and he began working at the lodge the next day.

*November 14–December 22 Christy's Lodge*

In the middle of the month, Freer attended some Christmas activities.

> *Dec 15* "Went to the Indian concert at the large school. It was very good."

> *Dec 16* "Everybody went to the Christmas concert at the Indian School and all report that it's very good." Freer also went to the concert at the public school two days later.

Freer visited the game warden on December 21 and got poison to take into the Kechika.

*December 23–December 31 Kechika River valley*

Freer flew with Dalziel from Watson Lake to Horneline Lake on December 23, a one-hour flight that cost $180. Christmas was uneventful. On December 27, Freer left Horneline Lake with a heavy pack. It took two days to reach Dust Cabin. Freer arrived at Cottonwood Flats on the last day of 1953.

## 1954

This would be a year in which Freer's activities took him away from the Kechika from the beginning of April to mid-November, and his packing extended from Vanderhoof to a new area of Yukon territory farther away from Lower Post.

*January 1–March 31 Kechika River valley*

> *Jan 1* "Well, this is the start of another year and shall see what it brings. I left Cottonwood Flats and arrived at Diamond J Ranch at noon. Skook was sure glad to see me."

On January 13, Freer went to Frank and Jack George's place and bought a sleigh from them for twenty-five dollars. He and Skook intended to use it for hauling hay.

> *Jan 17* "We tried the transmitter all day yesterday. Couldn't get out, but could hear several stations loud."

> *Jan 18* "We were on the transmitter all day, got through to Fort St. James at 4 PM. We got our wires out through Stewart at 5 PM. Well, we are in contact with the outside world now."

Christy's, Lower Post. Image F-06563 courtesy the Royal BC Museum and Archives

In his diary entry for January 28, Freer wrote that Skook had fallen on a log several days earlier and had severely hurt his ribs.

Freer left Skook's ranch on February 3 with the sleigh on his way to Horneline Lake. He arrived five days later where he noted that "the radio is sure booming in." Freer stayed at Horneline Lake for a few days.

*Feb 10* "Four wolves came down Horn Lake at just dark. I got a black one and wounded another but he kept going."

In mid-February, Freer took a second trip to Horneline Lake and brought back the rest of his stuff with the sleigh. Freer went to Horneline Lake twice in March. On the second trip, he found that "somebody left a pole standing against the cache and it is sure full of mice. All my grub is ruined."

*Mar 26* "I put everything away in the cache at Dust cabin as I am going to be away all summer.... I will be going out to Lower Post April 1."

*April 1–June 3 Christy's Lodge*

On the last day of March, Dalziel arrived early and Freer flew with him to Watson Lake, the fare $75.

> *Apr 1* "Very rough in the air. I was terribly sick.... I am working at Christy's at Lower Post in the store and at the gas pumps and other jobs at times. I sold the Indian fur at the HBC."

> *Apr 3* "Skook came in from Terminus Mountain yesterday. I saw him early this morning and he was sure drunk.... I gave Skook the Indian money all done up in a parcel and bills and everything." Skook flew back to his ranch on April 4.

April was a busy month at the lodge, with lots of truck traffic.

> *Apr 7* "I am working long hours as Flo [Christy] hasn't got any help yet."

During the summer of 1954, Freer packed for Northwestern Explorations again.

> *May 15* "G.A. Nosts came down from Whitehorse to meet Axel Berglund [a well-known prospector in the Yukon] and Walter Cannon who came from Prince George and are going into the headwaters of Hyland River to prospect. These two men will be here until 1 June."

Berglund was prospecting for copper. Fred Carlick was guiding the packer, Buster Groat, to the site. This was Northwestern's main project. There was also a second crew, for which Freer was packing, that worked at a site accessed from Mile 1117 on the Alaska Highway at Kluane River.

*June 3–September 14 Northwestern Explorations, Mile 1117, Alaska Highway*

In the afternoon of June 3, Freer loaded his seven head of horses, and he and Chris Edzerza, along with his wife, Lizzie, took this outfit to Mile 1117 on the Alaska Highway. They arrived the morning of June 5, and Freer forded the Kluane River to the horse camp on the west side.

> *June 7* "My horses pulled out on me and went up towards Kluane Lake. It was 1 AM when I got back without the horses."

The next day, Freer found the horses about twelve kilometres up the Kluane River. This was the first of several times when Freer's horses left camp. Two days later, Freer began packing food up to the main camp. It took seven and a half hours to make a round trip.

Freer spent the second half of June taking supplies up to the main camp and improving the trail. He still had trouble with the horses trying to leave.

*June 26* "The horses came in today for the first time since I took them downriver. But as soon as I turned them loose they headed up the river. They keep trying to get home."

During July, Freer packed supplies to the main camp. The horses continued straying from the horse camp. In late July, the bulldog flies became troublesome. Several times Freer had smudges going all day.

August started with more trouble from the horses.

*Aug 1* "I had to go clear through to Kluane Lake after my horses." Freer arrived back in camp at 2:00 a.m.

*Aug 26* "I have Rose, the leader, hobbled and that holds them."

*Sept 1* "Arrived in main camp at noon. Went down to the lake [Kluane] and brought up Jim Scott from Vancouver, Northwestern office, and Bill Miller from New York office. Gerry Nosts went in too. The plane returned to Whitehorse."

*Sept 2* "Went up to the main camp, took Jim Scott and Bill WD Miller and Gerry Nosts and they went out to Whitehorse at 5 PM with the plane. I brought Jim Rutherford's clothes and dunnage down and also Slim's stuff. Slim came down with me. Arrived in my Kluane camp at 10 PM."

*Sept 4* "The bosses went down Kluane River tonight. Jim Rutherford came down from the main camp and is going out and back to his home in Edmonton Alberta. He stayed the night here."

*Sept 5* "Jim Scott and Bill Miller came up and picked up Jim Rutherford at 11:30 AM."

Freer started packing items from the main camp back to the river camp on September 6. By September 9, he was finished. As a finale, six of Freer's horses went up the Kluane River and Willard did not return with them until midnight.

*Sept 10* "Loaded the horses and went into Whitehorse. The damn truck is sure haywire. It broke down." It took four days before Freer was able to leave Whitehorse, and he arrived at Lower Post on September 14.

*September 15–30 Travel to Fort St. James and preparations for trip to Diamond J*

On September 20, Freer got a ride in Christy's tanker that was going to Dawson Creek. Four days later, he arrived in Fort St. James. He spent a couple of days at the police warehouse fixing up some of his items, and "got my rigging ready to take north." Then he went to Erhorn's ranch and picked up his horses. On the last day of the month, Freer started travelling to the Kechika.

*September 30–November 15 Trip to Diamond J Ranch with Clem Reierson*

At Germansen Landing, on October 12, Freer picked up Clem Reierson to help him on the trip back to the Kechika. The twenty-one-year-old Reierson had been working on road construction in the area and hoped to see more of northern BC. Freer wanted someone to assist him on the long trip back to the Kechika since it was getting late in the season for travelling through a remote area.

In a book titled *From Vanderhoof to Lower Post*, Reierson recounted his adventures with Freer and Skook during his time with them from October 1954 to February 1955. Reierson dedicated the book to Wilf [Freer], and it is based on Clem's diaries. He wrote prosaically about some of the incidents briefly described in Freer's diaries, and he provided his perspective on Freer's personality.

On October 14, the two men departed, initially heading for Thutade Lake. They then followed the main trail to Fort Ware, arriving on November 2.

> *Nov 13* "We had a very good horse wrangle at City Cabins and went to Gataga River at the forks of Kechika and Gataga Rivers.... Gataga River is too full of floe ice to try to cross, so will cache everything here.... (End of the trail for the horses, thank my lucky stars.)"

> *Nov 14* Freer recorded that he and Reierson "put a pole bridge across the Gataga River where it is nearly jammed and put all of my outfit up in a cache."

The next day, the two men arrived at the ranch at 7:30 p.m. Reierson wrote:

> When we got close enough I could see a high arch with a sign on the top. I could just make out Diamond J Horse Ranch. It was built on a bridge that spanned a small creek. On a rise beyond the bridge stood the house with a dim light showing through a window. As we were walking up the rise, the door flew open and out came a black lab dog and right behind him Skook Davidson.

*November 16–December 31 Kechika River valley*

Reierson soon learned that there was no plane scheduled to pick him up, and with the river ice still moving, it was impossible for an aircraft to land. Reierson wrote: "It looks like I'm here for a while." Reierson worked with Skook on activities around the ranch while Freer did the cooking and indoor activities.

Freer and Reierson started for Horneline Lake on Christmas and started the return trip on December 30. They stayed at Dust Cabin that night and remained there on the last day of 1954 because the temperature was –40°C all day.

# 1955

*January 1–February 12 Kechika River valley; trip to Lower Post with Clem Reierson*

By January 3, Freer and Reierson were back at Dust Cabin. Reierson was anxious to return home, so Freer marked a plane landing near the cabin. Then Reierson returned to the Diamond J Ranch while Freer spent time at his cabin.

> *Jan 22* "Clem Reierson came down from Skook's Diamond J Ranch. He is in a great rush to get to Lower Post."

Freer went to Horneline Lake for a few days. At the end of January, Freer and Reierson prepared to travel to Lower Post, and they departed on February 2. They met Jack George returning from Lower Post. He had Freer and Reierson's mail.

> *Feb 11* The two men arrived at Lower Post in the early evening. That day "Fred and Annie Forsberg had a son, John Rudolph, born." Reierson departed on the bus the next day.

*February 12–March 12 Alaska Highway*

Freer noted that Christy's Lodge had been leased for five years by G.A. Wright. Jack Christy was going to Whitehorse with a load of gas and Freer accompanied him. While they were there, Freer visited Jerry Nosts of Northwestern Explorations. Freer also visited other mining companies but was unable to make any definite arrangements for the field season.

*March 12–May 25 Kechika River valley*

> *Mar 12* "Vic McGuire took me to Dust cabin with the Taylorcraft after dinner."

The Diamond J Ranch around 1955. This picture was used as the cover photo for Reierson's book, *From Vanderhoof to Lower Post*. Clem Reierson Family collection

Over the next four days, McGuire brought three loads of supplies. Then Freer went up to see Skook, returning to his cabin at the end of March. On April 1, Vic McGuire brought a load of grub and the mail in Dalziel's Taylorcraft airplane. Freer spent a few days with Skook and then went looking for his horses, which he hadn't seen for a while. He found them in the City Cabins area.

In early May, Freer cleaned out the trails around his area and cut firewood.

> *May 5* "I went to Starvation Creek and got a good fire going all along the valley between Horn Creek and Starvation."

> *May 6* "The fire sure did a very good job on the Horn Creek flats."

> *May 20* Freer left for Skook's place where he found Jack Abou, Jack and Frank George and Jimmy Massetoe. "Francis Charlie and son Alan Charlie are here from Fort Grahame for their beaver hunt." The men spent a few days getting organized.

*May 24* "I was busy cooking and sewing rigging. Skook worked on the rigging. The Indians wrangled the horses and fixed up their beaver. Jack Abou and Alan Charlie left for Fish Creek yesterday to make a couple of rafts for us to cross the river at 66 mile."

## May 25–June 1 Trip to Lower Post

On May 25, the men started their journey to Lower Post where Freer was supposed to meet Bronlund on June 1.

*May 27* "We had a good horse wrangle at Horn Creek and went through to Fish Creek where Jack Abou has built 2 rafts to take to 66 mile to cross the Muddy." They swam the horses and rafted the equipment across the river without difficulty the next day and arrived at Lower Post on June 1.

*June 1* "We left 17 mile and arrived at the Dease River. Swam the horses to McNab point. Was a very easy swim as there isn't any water in the river, still ice on the river shores. There is very little horse feed. We put our camp on McNab point. Skook went up town and proceeded to get drunk."

## June 1–July 11 Lower Post waiting for Emil Bronlund, CM&S

Freer stayed at Lower Post for several days.

*June 6* "Skook returned to camp at 7 AM at McNab point. He is sure damn sick too. He sure gave me a scare. He dropped and I had to help him to bed."

*June 7* The next day Alan Charlie, Frank and Jack George quit. "I have to stay in camp all the time. Skook is ill, pretty sick."

*June 10* Freer and Skook took "12 head of horses up to Mile 625 and packed a test radar up for the RCAF."

During his time camped around Lower Post, Freer's diaries mention drinking and fighting in several entries. Freer also noted that Skook was drunk for much of the time. On June 16, Freer fixed up Skook's supplies at the Hudson's Bay Company.

*June 17* "I am alone here now with 8 head of horses."

Freer remained at Lower Post for the rest of June, looking after the horses and doing some odds and ends.

*June 30* "I looked after my horses, went up town and did nothing. No sign of Bronlund as yet. I have spent a whole month here waiting, which is very tiresome." On July 2, he received a telegram from Bronlund stating that he wouldn't arrive until July 12.

*July 11* "Emil Bronlund arrived today at long last."

## *July 11–August 16 Packing for Emil Bronlund*

*July 13* "Bronlund took all the equipment out to 10 miles [16 kilometres] north of Watson Lake and left the trail there."

Bronlund travelled up Tom Creek into Yukon territory but couldn't find a trail. It rained for several days. One of the horses "went upside down in a creek and got everything wet. All dried stuff. Pretty tough going."

*July 22* "We laid over today and spread out that load to dry."

The next day Bronlund and Freer reached the first Tom Lake, but still hadn't found a trail. On July 26, they crossed over the Tom Creek summit and started down the Stewart Creek watershed. Two days later they arrived at Stewart Lake, and on July 30, they reached Oscar Lake. The crew continued going north and west. On August 6 and 7, there was heavy rain all day. "Everything is full of water now," Freer wrote. The next day Bronlund decided to return to Lower Post. On August 15, the men arrived at the Alaska Highway at Mile 630 and came on to Lower Post.

*Aug 16* Freer finished his work with Bronlund. "This was a damn poor year for me, only $920."

## *August 17–September 11 Lower Post and trip to Diamond J*

*Aug 19* "Got everything ready to go. I expect to cross the Liard and Dease rivers Sunday. All my grub was stolen at McNab point today. I don't know who did it.... I was quite sick today."

*Aug 20* "I am still sick. I was up town. The plane went out to Dall Lake with Skook's hunters."

*Aug 21* "I hired Frank Hollins to put all my outfit across the Liard and Dease rivers. I swam the horses at the Mission or Indian School, and it was a very good swim."

Freer started the return trip to the Kechika on August 23, with "7 fairly heavy loads." On September 1, he arrived at Horneline Lake at his lower place. Freer spent the first week of September doing a variety of chores.

> **Sept 9** Freer went to Dust Cabin. "Somebody has certainly ransacked my Dust cabin cache, took some grub out and left everything in a hell of a mess."

## September 11–23 Trip to Lower Post

On September 11, Freer went to the Diamond J Ranch. He noted that Skook had a new cabin and that his horses were in the meadow. Freer left with John Johnny and Jack Williams enroute to Lower Post. On September 17, the men took three raft trips across the Kechika River. On September 23, the men arrived at Dease River and Don Miller took them over to Lower Post.

## September 24–October 1 Lower Post

While he was at Lower Post, Freer got his land papers ready at John Dowsette's.

> **Sept 27** "John Dowsette and I left Lower Post and went into the Cassiar asbestos mine. I got my land papers fixed up."

Freer, Dowsette, and later, Skook, intended to purchase land from the BC government. For Freer and Skook, this land would be where they currently lived, while Dowsette wanted a parcel near Lower Post where he could live during retirement. It was expensive to have a registered BC land surveyor come to a remote area, so the government paid the costs. However, the purchaser had to wait until the BC government had a surveyor working on a project in the area. When Art Swannell (BCLS #288, and the son of Frank Swannell) was surveying in the Lower Post area for the BC government in 1960, he was also directed to survey the parcels of land these three men wanted to purchase.

## October 2–15 Return trip to Diamond J Ranch

The return trip started on October 2. Freer had Ernie Frank and Frank George to help him with twenty-three head of horses and fifteen packs.

> **Oct 8** They reached Mile 66 on the Kechika River. "We added 2 logs to my raft. We made one trip across the river."

> **Oct 9** "The boys moved everything across the river. We will just have our camp to move in the morning."

On October 10, they swam the horses across the river. On October 15, they arrived at the Diamond J Ranch where Freer saw about thirty sheep and three goats on the hill. The next day the men put everything away for Skook.

*October 16–December 31 Kechika River valley*

> *Oct 17* "Ernie Frank and I went up river and brought in a bunch of horses. Frank George made a raft to cross the river. We saw a large bunch of goats, sheep and deer together."

There were no visitors in November, and from November 21 to 26, the nighttime temperature was below –40°C every night.

On December 4, Ernie Frank arrived with mail from Lower Post, Freer's first visitor since October. He stayed until December 6. On December 17, Freer trapped a wolverine. That night it got below –40°C and nighttime temperatures stayed below until December 28.

> *Dec 25* "So damn cold, a person can't do much."

On the last day of 1955, Freer wrote about the cold in December but noted there was very little snow, with only about 7.5 centimetres on the ground.

# 1956

*January 1–May 17 Kechika River valley*

Freer started the new year by taking a second load of grub to the top of the hill toward Horneline Lake. On January 6 and 7, the nighttime temperature got below –40°C, and Freer spent much of his time packing in and cutting wood. Freer took his last load to the hilltop on January 10. Ernie Frank and Jack George came down from Skook's ranch the same day.

> *Jan 12* "Jack George left for his place heavily loaded with grub. Ernie Frank and I left for Horn Lake," arriving there on January 13.

Freer and Frank spent two weeks in the Rabbit River drainage. During the first week, they set traps and examined the condition of the cabins; then checked the traps during the second. On January 30, they arrived back at Horneline Lake. Freer had trapped two marten, two lynx, one fisher, one wolverine, one weasel and three squirrels during the month.

On February 8, Freer and Frank went to Dust Cabin. The next day, Frank went to Skook's, while Freer marked out a plane landing nearby.

> *Feb 14* "We had 2 fires going to stop the plane, but it never appeared." The temperature was –50°C that morning.

> *Feb 17* "Ernie Frank, Jack George, Frank George and Allan Charlie left for Lower Post with two dog teams."

Dalziel arrived in the afternoon of February 22 with the Cessna 180. Freer spent a couple of days taking loads of food to the top of the hill on the way to Horneline Lake. On February 28, Freer arrived at the lake with a heavy pack. A week later, he finished transporting his supplies to the lake. Freer spent two weeks on his trapline. By March 24, he was back at Dust Cabin. "The radio is good, and good to hear it as I have been gone a month."

> *Apr 6* "Ernie Frank, Jack and Frank George arrived back from Lower Post." Louis Boya came up from Fish Creek.

> *Apr 7* "Jack and Frank George got some grub from me and headed up river to trap beaver. Louis Boya got some grub and returned to his family at Fish Creek."

Two weeks later, Ernie Frank and Frank George came down and got a small quantity of food. Freer finished digging his garden on the last day of the month.

> *May 3* "I back fired around here all day."

> *May 5* Freer went to Skook's place. "Skook is looking old now."

A week later, Frank George stopped on his way to Lower Post with four pack dogs.

## May 17–26 Trip to Lower Post and preparation for packing

In mid-May, Freer got ready to head to Lower Post where he would be packing for Northwestern Explorations again. On May 17, Willard departed from Skook's with thirty-two head of horses. A week later, they swam the Dease and Liard Rivers and arrived at Lower Post. Dave Barr came to meet Freer on May 26.

## June 5–September 21 Packing for Northwestern Explorations' Flat Lake mineral claims

Freer left Lower Post on June 5. His destination was the Flat Lakes area in Northwest Territories where Axel Berglund had staked some mineral claims in 1954. This was Freer's only packing trip that covered both Yukon and Northwest Territories. By June 13, Freer was at the Hyland River, and he followed a route up this river for two weeks.

> *June 27* "Camped in an old survey camp on a lake on the river."

> *June 28* "Flagged a plane down and went into Watson Lake for some grub as I have been out for about 10 days. As soon as the

aircraft pilot saw the smoke he came right over and landed."

*June 29* "Dalziel was in at 7 AM with the Cessna 180 with grub for me. I gave him a quarter of caribou meat."

*June 30* "Am in open country. The river is very swift and bouldery."

*July 4* Freer finally arrived at the Flat Lakes. That afternoon he "made a flight in a helicopter to the drill site to look the route over."

Dave Barr described the mining operations: "Because of the distance between our proposed base camps and the Axel deposit, I had opted for a diamond drilling project supported by both helicopters and packhorses. This was to be provided by Skook Davidson at Terminus Mountain through Willard Freer."

The camp at Flat Lakes was a base camp for the drilling operations situated about eighteen kilometres away above the timber line. Supplies would be flown in from Watson Lake while Freer would do the packing between the camp and work site. A helicopter was used mainly for transportation of people. On July 12, Dick Campbell, Northwestern's head of operations for their Whitehorse office, arrived by helicopter to visit the drilling site.

*July 18* "Dave Barr came in, stayed at Summit Lake [a nearby lake]. Dick Campbell went out from Summit Lake."

*July 20* "Left Flat Lake with 2 loads of gas and 3 loads of grub, arrived at the drill camp at 7 PM. The helicopter was down and returned to Summit Lake, brought Dave Barr down and took him to the drill camp.... I stayed at the drill camp."

*July 25* "I took 3 loads of grub up to the drill camp and 2 loads of gas and returned with Dave Barr. Arrived back at 2 PM. It is sure a tough climb up to the drill camp." Barr noted that on the same day a ground fire caused extensive damage to the helicopter.

Dalziel flew in with a Beaver float plane on July 29 and August 8. He returned on August 10 with news that the drill camp was being disbanded. From August 17 to 19, a Pacific Western Junkers airplane moved the men and equipment out. Freer spent the final days cleaning up the camp in heavy rain.

*Aug 25* Freer started the return trip. "Arnold Frank and I left

Flat Lake at the head of Nahanni River and camped on the head of Hyland River. It is sure very tough going. I had three horses down in a mudhole."

*Aug 26* "I took the wrong creek and made a complete circle of a mountain.... Very wet all day."

*Aug 27* "Had a very good horse wrangle and left our camp on the East fork of the Hyland River and came over to the west fork of Hyland River to Brodell's hunting camp. The hunters are up at the head of the river. Mrs. Brodell is at the base camp."

Freer stayed at the hunting camp for two days because of heavy rain. On August 30, Freer and Frank left for Lower Post. Freer observed thirty to forty large flocks of cranes flying south on September 14. The two men arrived at Lower Post on September 21.

In describing the operations, Barr commented: "I was particularly pleased with the support of the diamond drilling crew at the Axel showing by a combination of the helicopter and Willard Freer and his horses." However, the season was not an economic success. "Our prospecting teams in 1956 found no showings worthy of staking except two... later determined to be of no economic interest, after more detailed examination."

Kennco allowed these claims to lapse. However, in late 1958, further exploration by another mining group called the Mackenzie Syndicate "resulted in the discovery of several occurrences of skarn-bearing scheelite in the Flat River area," Barr wrote. "Among these was the Axel showing, which was staked shortly after the expiry of Kennco's claims. The lack of recognition by Kennco of the tungsten content of the deposit is what Sullivan later referred to as the Flat River disaster." (John Sullivan was president of Kennco.)

This became the first major location of tungsten in western Canada. In 1959, the Canadian Tungsten Mining Corporation was incorporated. The Cantung mine operated for many years, and in the early 1980s, it was the largest producer of tungsten in North America. In 1995, Barr wrote: "After 40 years of exploration in the region we explored in 1955 and 1956, it is prophetic that the Axel showing, the first significant deposit recognized in the 14,000 square mile region explored by Kennco is the only one to have reached production." Interestingly, Freer would have a few small connections with Canadian Tungsten in future years.

*September 21–December 31 Lower Post*

While Freer was at Lower Post, he and a few other men received employment working on the Border Inn property, which the Wrights had bought. Freer arranged with Jack George and Amos Alec to take his horses back to the Kechika, and he moved everything across the Liard and Dease Rivers on October 8.

> *Oct 10* "We are all still working up at the Border Inn and is sure a slow job fixing up the old building. Nothing sits square. Snowed some."

> *Oct 20* "The old plant quit on us and so we are out of lights and all the business has stopped. We moved all of the Wrights furniture out of the hotel and cleaned out everything in the store."

> *Oct 22* "I worked here all day, on shovel, in the store and at everything. Grady Wright went to Whitehorse to see about a light plant. The boys got the old light plant running."

> *Nov 13* "We finished all the windows and the building is starting to look like something now. We have a new ceiling in the old building now too."

> *Nov 15* "The Watson Lake electricians have completed the wiring. It is good to have light again."

A disaster occurred in early December.

> *Dec 5* "Everybody is working inside and Don Miller just back from garage and says a fire has broken out, so it is a great jumble trying to put out the fire, but no luck, so we heaved everything outside that we could move. Some of the town people were up helping. Lost the Witte [diesel] engine $4000, lost 400 gallons diesel and garage, a lot of other equipment too.... Lorna and Mrs. Wright were out helping too. This was a great loss, around $10,000 fire. It is sure a great setback. Everybody was soaked to the eyebrow from water. Wright notified the insurance adjuster at Whitehorse right away. He cancelled the weekly grub order from Dawson Creek. Well, we have no lights now again. 2 months work gone up in smoke in less than an hour. It is sure a great loss to the Wrights as they were just getting started to bring in a little cash."

*Dec 6* "Nobody did much of anything today after the big fire yesterday.... It was pretty cold to be out so long. We were still throwing stuff out when the roof and ceiling was starting to fall in."

*Dec 7* "I am putting in long hours trying to get something done."

The rest of the month was uneventful. Freer described a quiet Christmas.

*Dec 25* "Nobody did anything all day. I did the usual chores. The Asp family were up after supper for the evening. Everybody had a good time and nobody had too much to drink."

*Dec 31* "I finished boarding up the bottom of the service station. I also sawed some wood and the other chores around the place. Well, this is the end of another year and hope the new year will bring better seasons."

# 1957

## January 1–February 18 Lower Post

At the beginning of 1957, Freer was working for the Wrights at Lower Post.

*Jan 1* "Henry, Herman, and mother Mrs. Asp were up for the evening. It was 4 AM when the party broke up." Through the rest of January, Freer did a variety of chores around the lodge.

In early February, Freer wrote that the Wrights had purchased a new power saw.

*Feb 6* "Grady [Wright] and I went to the nurse and had a shot each to see if we could get rid of colds." The next day they had another shot from the nurse.

*Feb 14* "Father Levaque took Fred Herbert up to the plane to go to the military Hospital at Vancouver. He had a heart attack a couple of days ago."

## February 18–May 27 Kechika River valley

Freer flew from Watson Lake to the Kechika River with George Dalziel and his Cessna 180 on February 18. He noted that there was about fifteen centimetres of snow at Dust Cabin.

*Feb 19* "The second plane came with the rest of my stuff." That afternoon Frank George came up from Starvation Creek, and the next afternoon "Louis Boya and family came up from Starvation."

*Feb 21* "I put the rest of the stuff away and put up my small tent. Louis and Minnie came up from Dust Creek where they are camped and got some groceries."

*Feb 22* "The Beaver plane went up river today. I guess they are out dropping poison for the wolves."

*Feb 24* Freer arrived at his destination. "The Horn Creek cabin has sure been cleaned out of grub. Dust cabin was sure cleaned out too." On the last day of the month, Freer wrote that he put out some poisoned meat.

Freer spent a couple of days visiting Skook in early March.

*Mar 3* "He is looking good but crippled bad."

On March 14, Freer went to Dust Cabin. Amos Alec, Louis Boya, and Frank and Jack George were there. A plane was supposed to come in with supplies, but it didn't arrive.

*Mar 15* "I got quite a bit of fur and sold quite a lot of grub," Freer wrote.

*Mar 16* "I hauled some wood and stretched a beaver that Frank George left. Restretched a fisher. Frank George was up from Dust Creek. I waited for the plane, but [it] never came." Freer had plans to rebuild his cabin, so while he was waiting for the airplane, he shovelled snow and hauled some wood to the location.

*Mar 19* "Stan Bridcut went up the valley with his super cub and returned and stopped in for coffee. I sent the mail out with Stan. No sign of Dalziel yet. This is 5 days I have waited."

On March 24, the plane finally arrived with Freer's supplies. Frank George went up to Skook's and took the mail with him. He returned on March 29 with one beaver that he trapped. The next day, he stretched the beaver at Dust Cabin where Freer was staying.

In early April, Freer went up to Skook's place to visit him before he began working on his new cabin. The ice and snow were melting, so Freer marked out a new plane landing on April 6.

*Apr 7* "The plane came in on time for a change. Bill Williams and Jim Monetts came, and some grub. I put the grub in the cache here. The boys went up to Skook's."

Louis Boya and Frank George came up from Fish Creek on April 11.

*Apr 12* "Louis Boya and Frank George went down to Starvation Creek. Jim Monetts was down from Skook's and returned. I took a load of grub down to Horn Creek on the ice. No snow on the ice. I saw the horses at Horn Creek. There is about an inch [2.5 centimetres] of green grass where the horses are on the hills."

Freer continued working on his cabin throughout April.

*May 24* Freer met Bill Williams at Dust Creek. "Skook has hurt himself quite bad, so he will not be going to Lower Post." Freer arrived at the Diamond J late in the evening. Two days later, he got ready to take Jim Monetts and Bill Williams to Lower Post.

## May 27–July 3 Alaska Highway

The men left Horneline Creek on May 27. At Fish Creek, Jack and Frank George joined them. On June 1, they arrived at Lower Post. There were no job offers in the mail, so Freer went to Watson Lake to see if he could find any work. While Freer was waiting and hoping to get work, he helped at the Wright's lodge in Lower Post.

## July 3–September 4 Packing for Continental Mining

Freer finally got some work for his horses on July 3 packing for Continental Mining. The next day, he loaded them onto a truck and took them to Mile 687 at Lower Rancheria in Yukon. On July 6, he headed north, following a cat trail. Three days later he came to the Liard River and crossed at a place where the current was slow and the water was not too deep. He made a raft and took two trips across the Liard, then swam the horses across and continued up the river.

By July 12, Willard was at Wasson Lake. The plane came in three times with supplies. There were five men and three horses. The next day, Freer went up to the Wasson Lake claims with five head of horses. It took him about ten hours to reach the site. On July 15, he moved the cook tent and the rest of the men up to the claims. Freer went up to the main camp near the claims on July 26.

During August, Freer was busy packing goods to a couple of different locations where the men were working on claims. By mid-August, the work was finished, and Freer began packing out the men and equipment.

*Aug 19* "The Conwest plane arrived and Al Storey and Art Lake went out with a load. The Newmont plane was in twice. The Bombardier was down from the drill camp. Fairly clear. I brought in the horses from the east end of Wasson Lake."

The next day, Freer finished cleaning up the camp, and on August 21, he returned to Wasson Lake. On August 26, Freer departed. He followed the cat trail back to the Alaska Highway, arriving on the last day of the month. Freer travelled with the horses along the Alaska Highway to Lower Post.

*Sept 2* "Lots of people took pictures of my outfit." Hans Anderson took Freer's loads to Watson Lake, making Freer's return trip quicker.

## September 4–October 13 Alaska Highway

Freer arrived in Lower Post on September 4 and spent time working at the Wright's lodge. Most of Freer's work was outdoors, hauling wood for the winter and cleaning up the grounds around the lodge.

On October 9, Freer and Frank George crossed the Liard River. The men were sick, so they didn't start travelling to the Kechika until October 13.

## October 13–26 Travel to Freer's cabin at Horneline Creek

Amos Alec, his daughter, and John Johnnie caught up to Freer three days later. On October 17 and 19, Amos Alec helped him pack up. Freer followed Alec's trail toward Turnagain River and went up the west side of the Kechika. When Freer reached the mouth of Horneline Creek, he found that the back channel was frozen, and he had to make a brush bridge.

*Oct 25* "I led the horses across this brush bridge. The ice sure did lots of cracking. Forded the main channel." On October 26, Freer arrived at his cabin on Horneline Creek.

## October 26–December 9 Kechika River valley

Freer spent time cleaning and putting away items from his summer work. He also worked on his new cabin through November.

*Nov 13* "I finished putting the lumber on the roof and got it trimmed too."

*Nov 15* "I finished putting up the roof. It is some patch work."

*Nov 16* "I put 2 windows in today. It is a slow job as everything has to be re-fitted or built up."

*Nov 18* "I finished putting in the windows and odds and ends around."

On November 25, Freer met Skook at Cottonwood Flats. The next day he went to the Diamond J Ranch with Skook. Amos Alec and Jack George came over from Turnagain River. On November 28, Freer left Skook and went to Dust Cabin. Freer moved into his cabin on December 1.

### December 10–18 Trip from cabin to Lower Post

Freer left his Horneline Creek cabin on December 10 and arrived at Lower Post eight days later. The temperature was mild and there was not much snow, so he didn't have to use snowshoes for the first week.

*Dec 18* "The Dease and the Liard Rivers are not frozen yet. I had to go all way down river to cross over. The Wrights were glad to see me. Their light plant is broke down."

### December 18–31 Lower Post

Freer was sworn in as an assistant postmaster for Lower Post while Mrs. Wright went out on a short holiday.

*Dec 23* "Went to a Christmas concert at the Indian School which was very good. There was sure a very large crowd there."

*Dec 25* On Christmas day it was –40°C. "Mrs. Bates and her two children were here for the day. Rev. Wheeler was in for dinner. A couple going to Alaska had dinner in the café. Very quiet. No liquor at all." On December 27, Mrs. Wright and her daughter departed by plane, heading for Los Angeles.

## PROJECT REINDEER

Father Yvon Levaque was principal and administrator of Lower Post Residential School during the late 1950s and early 1960s. In his diaries, Freer mentions meeting him a few times. At Lower Post, Father Levaque established a unique Christmas program called "Project Reindeer," which started in 1958. On the internet, the Prince George Digitization project, a collection of historical newspapers digitized by the Prince George Public Library, has several articles describing Christmas celebrations at this residential school.

On December 14, 1959, the *Citizen* published a front-page article titled "Santa Flies 610 Miles [976 kilometres] to Northern Christmas Party."

A twin-engine U.S. Air Force C-47 took off from Prince George early today carrying Santa Claus on a 610 mile [976 kilometre] flight into the north.

This evening, the white-whiskered gentleman will open his big sack of gifts for 186 Indian youngsters at the Indian Residential School at Lower Post, on the British Columbia-Yukon boundary.

Accompanying Santa are personnel from the U.S. Air Force base at Baldy Hughes, who have made the unique Christmas Stocking flight possible; representatives from the Prince George Lions Club, which is co-sponsor of the event; and newspapermen from the *Citizen* and the *Vancouver Sun*.

Known officially as Project Reindeer, the cargo will be flown to Watson Lake, 610 miles north of here, then trucked 16 miles [26 kilometres] to the Lower Post school.

There the delegation will be met by the school's principal, Father Yvon Levaque, who has arranged a Christmas party for the youngsters tonight.

This is the second year for Project Reindeer. It began when the Lions Club and the Baldy Hughes airmen, in response to an appeal from Father Levaque for anything that would make Christmas brighter for his little flock, decided to sponsor the school.

As a result of requests from Major Ken Coleman at Baldy Hughes, USAF sent up the aircraft Sunday. It touched down here at 1 PM following a 508 mile [813 kilometre] flight from Geiger Field at Spokane, Wash.

By 8 AM today, the airmen were busy stowing the Christmas packages in the plane and preparing for takeoff at 9:30 AM. Return trip will be flown tomorrow afternoon.

A front-page article on December 19, 1962, titled "Children again dub 'Reindeer' Smashing Success," described the fifth Christmas celebration. It noted that "the youngsters had a few surprises ready for the visitors, too. These took the form of an hour-long fascinating display of traditional Indian dances presented in the school's spacious gymnasium, complete with tom-toms and accoutrements and colorful, authentic costumes—made, incidentally, by the children themselves. A second treat for the visitors was a Christmas concert—the Indian's version of the Nativity—the students staged in the evening just before Santa made his appearance."

Father Levaque left Lower Post in the mid-1960s, but Project Reindeer continued for sixteen years, with its last program in 1973. A *Citizen* article titled "Lower Post Rejects Operation Reindeer" on December 3, 1974, explained the situation.

In a letter to the Lions, Father E. Morisset, administrator of the Lower Post Student Residence said the 'mentality of the Indian community is changing rapidly' and suggested the time had come to discontinue the program....

Father Morisset said the enrollment at the school has dropped to 75 this year, and predicted a "phasing out" of the residence in another two years.

"I have a feeling that our mission as a residential school has been accomplished and we should encourage the parents to accept their responsibilities more and more," he said.

Christmas concert at Lower Post Residential School in 1962. 86_38_9, Yukon Archives

"I shall write to the parents to encourage them to present their children with Christmas gifts," he said, adding "many parents are already doing this."

Father Yvon Levaque was invested with the Order of Canada in 1987; his investiture stated: "this retired priest has served Indian communities in the Canadian North with dedication for more than 40 years."

# 1958

*January 1–March 11 Lower Post*

Freer noted the start of one of the popular winter activities along the Alaska Highway.

*Jan 5* "Bud Wright went to Watson Lake to curl."

*Jan 8* "Everybody was in for the mail."

The arrival of the mail provided an opportunity to socialize with other people in the community. Mrs. Marjorie Bates, one of the public school teachers at Lower Post, invited Freer and Bud Wright for a turkey dinner on Sunday, January 12.

Freer was busy in his temporary position as assistant postmaster.

*Jan 15* "Had two mails to look after, and quite a bit in the first one."

*Jan 18* "The mail was in from the south and most of the people were in for the mail."

*Jan 23* "Made out the post office report."

*Jan 30* "Father [Yvon] Levaque brought over the battery that had been left to be charged."

Mrs. Bates invited Freer for Sunday dinner again on February 2, and he had a call from Mrs. Wright, who was in Waco, Texas. In February, Bud Wright went to curling bonspiels at Swift River and Coal River. Mrs. Bates and her children visited Freer almost every Sunday.

*March 11–May 26 Kechika River valley*

On March 4, Freer planned to fly home, but he had to wait a week before he was able to make the plane trip.

*Mar 11* "Well, I finally made it home. Father Levaque took me to the airport. Jack George, Amos Alec and Elsie Alec were here waiting for me. Jerry Davis flew to Skook's for the night." Unfortunately, Freer had a cold and was sick for several days.

Stan Bridcut flew in with Buster Groat on March 21, and Buster stayed for the night.

*Mar 22* The "Indians were all up to listen to the radio."

*Mar 23* "Four of the Porter boys were up from Fish Lake and returned. Amos Alec, Elsie Alec and Jack George went to Starvation. I loaned Amos my dog for a week. Elsie is going to stay at Starvation."

*Mar 26* Freer checked his horses and found them in good shape. "They sure were glad to see me."

*Mar 27* "Stan Bridcut came in looking for Buster Groat. Stan circled Cottonwood Flats, saw Buster and Stan stayed the night with me." The following morning, the two men left for Lower Post.

Freer had several visitors in April, including Amos Alec, Louis Boya, and Jack and Frank George. They were mainly bringing in fur from trapping to barter for supplies.

Freer noted on May 19 that there was a large fire up the river and lots of smoke in the Turnagain River valley.

*May 21* "That fire north of Starvation is sure burning to beat hell."

*May 23* Freer wrote again about the fire: "There will be nothing left there now." During the following weeks, forest fires burned a sizeable amount of the area.

*May 24* "The whole country is on fire. Sure is damn smoky, can see nothing at all."

### May 26–June 3 Trip to Lower Post

Freer got his outfit ready to go to Lower Post on May 26. Like the previous year, he had been unable to secure summer employment during the winter.

*June 1* The men reached Lower Post. "Swam the horses and put everything across the river. The Dease and Liard rivers are very low. There is a forest fire on the trail south of the Liard River. The Forestry have about 20 men out to fight it."

*June 4–July 15 Lower Post*

On June 4, Freer began working at the Wright's lodge. Freer continued to work at the lodge until he finally received employment on July 15.

*July 15–July 27 Work for George Midgley in Dease Lake area*

> *July 15* "Seymour was down with two fellows and want four head of horses for about two weeks east of Dease Lake." This was for George Midgley, a prominent mining engineer in northern BC and the territories, who was staking some claims in the area.

> *July 16* Freer went to Dease Lake on Midgley's truck. There "George Edzerza and I made a pen for the boat to take the horses to the south end of Dease Lake."

The next day, after a three-hour trip, the men arrived at a cat road that they followed for about eight kilometres. It took a week for Freer to reach the camp at the claims. Freer had only been there for a few days when there was a sudden change in plans.

> *July 27* "I moved the camp down from the claims on Midge Creek onto Eagle Lake. Was 2 hours. Petterson was in from Atlin and went on Gabrielse's camp. I have a job with Gabrielse now. My job with Midgley was ended today with cheque for $264 12 days."

## Hu Gabrielse

Hu "Gabe" Gabrielse was born in Golden, BC, in 1926. He graduated from Lord Tweedsmuir High School in 1944 and attended UBC, where he obtained a BA (1948) and an MA (1950) in geology. John Wheeler, an older friend and fellow geology student at UBC, went to Columbia University in New York City for his PhD, and Gabrielse decided to follow the same pathway. While at Columbia, he met Jean Freeman from New Jersey, and they married in 1955, the same year that Hu completed his PhD.

In the summer of 1947, Gabrielse was hired as a student assistant for a geological mapping program. This marked the beginning of Gabrielse's forty-six-year career with the Geological Survey of Canada (GSC), with all his fieldwork occurring in northern BC, and Yukon and Northwest Territories. In 1950, Gabrielse became a party chief and began working on the geology of the McDame area in northwestern BC, a project that would take several years. In 1953, he became a full-time employee of the GSC. Initially he was based in Ottawa, travelling to northern BC for summer fieldwork. He usually had about four student assistants and would hire a local packer and cook. Local plane service would bring in supplies about every two weeks.

Hu Gabrielse in the field. Hu Gabrielse Family collection

For the Geological Survey of Canada's mapping program, the geologist would map the features of the local landscape. Aerial photographs, the backbone for the fieldwork, would be used to identify their location. Back in the office, the aerial photographs would be matched to the federal government's 1:250,000 topographic maps, and a geological map would be produced, covering the same area as the topographic map. It usually took multiple summers in the field to cover the area included in one topographic map.

In 1956 and 1957, Gabrielse was involved in Operation Stikine, a large geological mapping project led by Dr. Fred Roots and the first systematic attempt to map the northern portion of the Canadian cordillera. In 1958, Gabrielse started his own geological mapping project, working east across northern BC. When he reached the Turnagain River area, Gabrielse hired Freer. Hu employed Willard during the 1958 to 1961 field seasons, and he was the local employee who worked the most summers for Gabe. Gabrielse recalls that Freer was a very versatile and reliable member of the crew: a packer and guide who knew the topography of the area and had his own horses. Freer also had a riverboat, which facilitated travel, particularly when Gabrielse mapped in the Kechika and Rabbit River drainages. In addition, Freer was able to work on the field crew when needed, could cook, and could provide fresh meat and fish. Gabrielse later employed Freer for part of the 1965 field season.

Gabrielse is well-known among geologists for his studies and over a hundred published papers on the northern cordillera. In 2000, the Geological Association of Canada, Canada's most prestigious geoscientific organization, presented him with the Logan medal, its highest award given annually to one individual. Gabrielse Cone in the Tuya Volcanic Field in the Stikine Mountains of northern BC is named for him.

Hu's wife, Jean, was cook for Gabrielse's crew for two summers, and they brought their son along. He wanted a big hat like Willard's, which they found on their next shopping trip to Whitehorse. Hu Gabrielse Family collection

## July 28–August 5 Travel to Denetiah Lake

This was a fortuitous situation for Freer. Hu Gabrielse was at the beginning of a multi-year geological mapping program for the Geological Survey of Canada in northern BC, and he needed a packer who knew the terrain of the Kechika River valley and surrounding area. Gabrielse provided four summers of employment for Freer before his mapping project moved out of the area. Gabrielse's mapping covered a large amount of terrain. Helicopters were used to transport the crew members to the different locations where they worked. Freer's horses moved camp. Supplies were flown by airplane to the lake nearest to the area where the men were working. Freer would then pack the goods to the campsite. Freer's riverboat was used on the Kechika and Rabbit Rivers to transport supplies and people.

Freer began travelling to Gabrielse's camp on July 28. Much of the route was along the Turnagain River. Freer arrived at Gabrielse's main camp at Denetiah Lake on August 5.

## August 5–September 6 Packer for Geological Survey of Canada

*Aug 8* "Gabrielse and I left Denetiah Lake with 9 horses, 3 light loads. Went to Dall Lake, moved on over a pass and camped at timberline. We are on the Kechika River trail. Saw lots of game. Lots of horse feed. Sure tough climbing today."

The two men remained at this camp for a second night while Gabrielse did his geological mapping. On August 10, Gabrielse completed his work in the area while Freer travelled toward the Kechika River valley and set up at one of Skook's camps. The next day Freer moved to another of Skook's camps where they stayed for three days.

*Aug 16* "Gabrielse and I arrived at West Moodie Lake at 1 PM, 3 horses." Three days later, Freer and Gabrielse left the lake and arrived at Denetiah Lake at dark on the following evening.

## September 6–14 Travel in Kechika River valley

*Sept 6* "I was 5 hours getting my horses and one still missing. The plane came in at 1:30 PM and Gabrielse went out. I got no clothes at all or grub."

*Sept 7* "I camped at the south end of Dall Lake. The plane came in at 1:30 PM and returned to Watson Lake. They were supposed to have grub and my clothes here at Dall Lake."

*Sept 13* "I left my camp on Sandpile Creek and went down the Turnagain River to the Kechika or Muddy River."

*September 14–October 8 Hunting guide for Amos Alec*

> *Sept 14* "Amos Alec was down from Porter Lake and wants me to go with him for about three weeks as he hasn't enough horses and Louis Boya quit him, so I will be taking my five horses for about three weeks hunt."

> *Sept 15* "Amos Alec and I left Porter Lake with eight pack loads and five saddle horses. We camped up Sandpile Creek at Amos's old hunting camp."

They set up camp the next day. Alec's clients were John Caputo from New York and John LaRocca, who was reputed to be a Mafia crime boss, from Pittsburgh, Pennsylvania. Caputo came on hunting trips to northern BC for several years. The men initially hunted for grizzly and bighorn sheep and were successful. In late September, they "got to the goat and caribou country" where they "saw lots of sheep and two caribou."

> *Oct 5* The men "moved to Porter Lake.... It was dark by the time I got here. Well, the job is done now. Very stormy and cold with some very heavy snowflakes."

The next day, Dalziel's Beaver plane arrived and took out the hunters and the women who cooked at the camps. Dalziel returned on October 8 at 10:00 a.m. and took Amos and Freer to Watson Lake.

*October 8–15 Watson Lake*

> *Oct 12* "Ernie [Frank] came in today with the horses. They are sure in wonderful shape. I will feed them hay tonight."

> *Oct 15* "Ernie Frank and I packed up, forded the Dease River and went to 6 mile."

*October 15–26 Travel to Freer's cabin*

> *Oct 17* "There are plenty of planes flying around looking for Fred Carlick's family around the head of the Stikine River."

Freer's October 22 entry provided grim news.

> *Oct 22* "Stan Bridcut stopped at Porter Lake yesterday and they found Fred Carlick dead at Chickshide Lake. Apparently he has been dead since August. Skook has 3 horses there fully rigged out and is too late to get the horses out now. They were on a Bralorne prospecting party. The horses

will have to be shot. Ernie and I moved all my outfit down to the Muddy at the mouth of Turnagain River."

After a day's rest on October 24, Freer "crossed the Turnagain River and followed the railroad survey up river." (Axel Wenner-Gren was a Swedish industrialist. In the 1950s, he made a proposal to the BC government for a railway that would go from BC to Alaska through the Kechika valley. The proposal generated considerable interest and controversy but minimal results.)

Freer forded the Kechika at Dust Cabin on October 26. He was home after an adventurous field season.

### October 26–December 31 Freer's cabin

*Oct 29* "Ernie and I took the government horses up to Skook's. It was dark when we got there. Frank George was there. Skook is sure looking old. His radio battery is on the bum." After spending a day with Skook, Freer and Ernie Frank returned to Dust Cabin.

During November, Freer was busy with activities around his cabin. On the last day of the month, Freer wrote that he marked out a plane landing on the river. He noted that the landing finally froze on December 7.

In December, Freer worked on digging out a cellar and building a new toilet.

*Dec 22* "The Beaver plane arrived with a load of supplies for me. Ernie Frank went out. I put all the stuff away." The next day Freer bought three lynx and one marten.

*Dec 25* "This is another Christmas gone. I had Amos Alec and daughter Emma and Jack George up for Christmas dinner. I didn't do too much but cook today."

*Dec 26* "Jack George and Amos Alec bought supplies. They expect to leave tomorrow for Turnagain River via Moodie Lakes and on the Dall River and Dall Lake."

*Dec 27* "Amos Alec and daughter Emma along with Jack George left for Dall River on Turnagain River via Moodie Lakes." Near the end of December, Freer put up a new radio aerial.

*Dec 31* "Looked at my traps and not a track of anything."

# 1959

*January 1–March 4 Kechika and trips to Lower Post*

From January 1 to 6 it was –40°C or colder every night, and Freer spent much of his time cutting and hauling wood.

> *Jan 9* "Stan Bridcut came in this morning. Don Miller was with him. They had breakfast here. Ran into a heavy snowstorm, had to land on small lake, got stuck in overflow. Snowed some with a north wind. They went on to Skook's and then up the Turnagain to Amos Alec's."

Freer received a radio message from Watson Lake airport on February 6 that Bud Wright wanted him to come into town during the curling bonspiel. Bridcut made a flight to Skook's ranch four days later, and he stopped at Freer's on the return to Lower Post.

> *Feb 18* Bridcut arrived and Freer went back to Lower Post with him. "Jack George is looking after my dog and is heading for Dall River tomorrow."

Stan Bridcut refueling airplane. In the late 1950s, Stan Bridcut started Watson Lake Flying Service. WLFS did most of the airplane flights into the Kechika. Hu Gabrielse Family collection

The next day, Bud Wright left for Whitehorse for a curling bonspiel. Freer was busy at the lodge, but in the evening, he visited people and played cribbage. The next weekend, Wright went to the Teslin Lake bonspiel.

### March 4–June 5 Freer's cabin

In early March, Freer returned to his cabin. He spent time checking on the horses, then on March 12, he went to Skook's place.

> *Mar 12* "His radio battery is gone, but I took up a new one. He hasn't any wood, he packs in enough every day."

Freer arrived back at his own cabin three days later. On March 24, Bridcut arrived with Freer's mail. Willard went to the Diamond J Ranch on March 28 with a heavy pack and stayed two nights. On the second day, Bridcut arrived and had lunch.

> *Apr 6* "Stan Bridcut was in today, went up to Skook's, stopped here and Scoop Lake, went up to the Turnagain. He had Amos Alec with him. Amos is going to trap beaver with his dad, Alec Chief." Bridcut returned on April 8 and stayed for the night on his way to Vancouver.

In May, Freer had transactions with some of the Indigenous trappers and a few trips to the Diamond J with oats and salt for Skook.

> *May 24* "Gerry Davis and his wife came in from Lower Post with their super cub plane and stayed for the night. Don Taylor and Bud Simpson came in with Taylor's Taylorcraft on wheels. They were sure lit up. Landed in the meadow. I did the cooking."

The next day, Davis dropped Freer off near his cabin. Freer stretched four beaver for Jack George. On May 27, George and Douglas Reid came down from Frog River. They swamped in the river and lost everything but their fur. The next day, George and Reid stretched their beaver.

Freer waited for a plane to come in on May 29, but it did not arrive.

> *June 3* "There will be a plane in looking for me very soon as I was supposed to be in by first of June for my party." Jerry Davis finally arrived at noon on June 5 and had lunch with Freer. "We left at 2:15 p.m., arrived Watson Lake at 9:15 PM, arrived at Lower Post at 3 AM."

*June 6–September 3 Packer for Geological Survey of Canada*

> *June 6* On his first day with the Geological Survey, Freer "worked around town all day and on the boat too. Went to Watson Lake. Saw Gabrielse. The boys are all going out to-day to my place to make camp."

It took a couple of days to get organized, and on June 9, Gabrielse flew into the Kechika River valley to get the first camp set up. This year much of Gabrielse's geological mapping was around the Kechika valley, so Freer's riverboat was a vital part of the transportation. It took Freer a couple of days before boat repairs were finished and the final supplies organized.

> *June 13* "We loaded up and landed on south side of Liard River."

Two days later, they arrived at Gabrielse's camp eight kilometres north of Dust Cabin. The following day, the crew moved up to Gataga Forks.

> *June 18* "Gabrielse and Robin Dalziel went to Skook's with us."

The next day, they cleared out a plane landing site, and a Cessna 180 came in with a crew from the Water Rights branch. Stan Bridcut and Jim MacDougall flew in with a super cub plane and stayed overnight on June 20. Freer and Adsit worked on boat repairs all day.

Gabrielse's initial work for the season was in the Gataga River area. On June 24, the men moved camp up the Gataga River. At their new location, they cleared out a helicopter landing site and started taking some of Gabrielse's crew to their work area. On June 26, Freer and Adsit worked on the boat all day while the helicopter took two trips in the afternoon bringing in the rest of the crew. The next day Bridcut flew in with boat parts for Freer.

During the first half of July, Gabrielse mapped the area west of the Kechika. The helicopter flew almost every day moving crew, and the Beaver plane took supplies to Denetiah Lake. On July 19, Freer moved camp to City Cabins farther up the Kechika, and the Cessna 180 brought in gasoline. Freer continued to have trouble with his boat. On July 21, he and Adsit put a new strut bearing in.

> *July 22* "Broke the inboard motor and came back down and something went wrong with the kicker, so I'm going to get the horses and pull out the boat here."

The next day, Freer and Robin Dalziel went to Skook's place. They built a raft at Gataga and travelled down the river. Freer picked up his horses at his place on July 24 and took them up to the main camp. He now had fifteen horses altogether. Near the end of July, Freer moved camp to Grizzly Creek farther up the Kechika, and Gabrielse mapped the area to the west. On August 4, they moved back to City Cabins.

In mid-August, Gabrielse mapped the area east of the Diamond J Ranch and through to the Rabbit River drainage. which mainly paralleled the Kechika. On August 23, Freer moved camp to his cabin on Netson Lake. Three days later, he travelled to the headwaters of the Caribou River and Rabbit River. While scouting the trail ahead, Freer came to one of Lash Collison's main camps.

> *Aug 27* "We saw Lash Collison and his party at his hunting camp."

> *Sept 2* "Had a good move from head of Rabbit River over summit to the head of Lue Creek. Camped in one of Collison's camps. Started to snow and rain. It was a steep climb." The next day, Freer took Gabrielse and his crew to Muncho Lake.

### September 6–16 Travel and return to Freer's cabin

Freer started his return trip on September 6. Four days later, he was at his cabin on Netson Lake. By September 12, he was at the Diamond J Ranch and returned to his cabin on September 14.

### September 17–October 3 Hunting guide for Robin Dalziel and return to Freer's cabin

Freer spent two days at his cabin before heading to Dall Lake on September 17 to work on a hunting party. Freer arrived on September 19, but Robin Dalziel's party was not there. On September 23, he left and went to the mouth of Dall River. From there he went to Porter Lake and reached Amos Alec's headquarters for his hunting camp on September 25. Freer picked up his mail and set up camp. Three days later, Amos Alec arrived back from a hunting trip with John Caputo.

### October 3–December 31 Freer's cabin

On October 1, Freer left Porter Lake, and by October 3, he was back at his cabin. The next day Davis was in three times, and he made two more trips the following day.

> *Oct 5* "I have all my grub now and about 800 pounds [365 kg] of oats here."

Freer went to Skook's place with the oats on October 10 and stayed there for three days. He spent most of the second half of October working around his cabin.

*Nov 17* "Jack George bought a bunch of grub for himself, Amos Alec and Louis Boya. Jack will return to Turnagain River tomorrow."

On November 22, Freer went to Cottonwood Flats and saw several horses along the way. He stayed overnight. Freer cut the trail up to Skook's on November 24. That night he met Frank George, who had shot three wolves with a rifle that Freer had loaned him. On November 26, Freer returned to his cabin, accompanied by George, who stretched the three wolves there.

*Dec 3* "Louis Boya came over from Amos Alec's on Turnagain River. Took out over 100 pounds [45 kilograms] of supplies and started back today. Frank George is going over with him." On December 11, George returned from Turnagain River. The next day, he shot a large fisher and caught a beaver.

*Dec 21* At Cottonwood Flats, "the Beaver plane from yesterday was in the meadow with a Christmas party from Watson Lake. Mrs. Rita Lund, Ted Ball, Bob Harrison the pilot. Hal and wife and 2 children. Skook was sure drunk. The party left at 3:30 PM for Watson Lake. There was sure plenty of liquor. Two search and rescue planes from Prince George went to Watson Lake and returned looking for a small plane that is down somewhere on this route. Skook has all his mail and he sure is sick now.... Stan Bridcut went to Lower Post flying high."

For Christmas, Freer cooked a chicken and Frank George came up for supper. On December 29, Bridcut flew in with Freer's mail and went to Skook's place and Amos Alec's. Freer spent the last day of 1959 doing odds and ends around the cabin.

# The 1960s: 1960–1969

## Highlights

By this decade, the era of the big pack trains was almost finished. Freer packed for the Geological Survey of Canada in the 1960 and 1961 field seasons. He spent most of the summers from 1962 to 1969 as a packer and a hunting guide for guide outfitters in the Kechika River valley and area.

In the 1960s, Freer started to spend more of his time working at Fireside, an Alaska Highway lodge near the junction of the Kechika and Liard Rivers. Freer also began learning how to construct and operate riverboats, and he used them for work and for travel between Fireside and his cabin. Freer maintained his trading with the Indigenous inhabitants of the Kechika River valley and spent almost every spring trapping season there.

## 1960

### January 1–May 27 Kechika River valley

In January, Freer worked on his cabin and built a cache. He also sawed some wood. Frank George came to visit several times. George shot a moose on January 2 and a deer on January 14. On January 7, Freer went to check his horses. He found all of them but noted that seven wolves passed through the area. The presence of wolves continued through February.

> *Feb 8* "Sure is a lot of wolf sign. They haven't touched my horses yet."

> *Feb 9* "I heard the wolves again today up Dust Creek."

> *Feb 19* "The BC-Yukon Beaver went north with Barry Paul and Bud Ellis, game wardens, putting out wolf baits."

> *Feb 24* "I went to Cottonwood Flats. There are sure lots of wolf signs."

> *Feb 25* "I chased the wolves all day but could not get within rifle range at all. They have killed 3 moose and 5 deer that I found."

> *Feb 26* "Went to Skook's place by way of the lake. Saw gov-

Around 1960, Freer started to use riverboats to travel up the Kechika to his cabin. Freer learned how to operate and construct riverboats. With their powerful motors, a trip up the Kechika could be made in one or two days depending on the amount of cargo being transported. The trip downstream took less than one day. The *Kechika Rose* was one of the riverboats that Freer built. Windrem Family collection

> ernment bait on the lake, ravens feeding on it and throwing. The paper is still there.... Skook says the wolves have killed four horses. Sheep on the hill. Stan Bridcut came from Fort Ware and went to Lower Post. I picked up the parcel that he left in the meadow."

*Feb 28* "Shot a coyote on the government bait."

Freer continued his fur-trading with the Indigenous residents of the Kechika. There are several entries detailing his visitors and their transactions.

> *Mar 1* "Jack George and Elsie Alec came over from the Turnagain River. They brought over just a bit of fur. They bought quite a bit of grub."

> *Mar 2* "Jack George and Elsie Alec left for Turnagain River. Louis Boya and Charlie Porter arrived here at midnight from

Porter Lake. They returned to Porter Lake. Frank George was up.... Sold a lot of groceries."

*Mar 29* "Jack George arrived here from the Turnagain River. He will be going up the Frog River very soon."

*Mar 30* "Jack George is repairing his sleigh. Stan Bridcut came in with a load of oats and returned to Lower Post by way of Turnagain River to pick up Margaret Abou to take her to Lower Post."

*Mar 31* "Stan Bridcut left for Vancouver today. He stopped here and had a lunch. Jack George got some grub. He was up river a ways and returned."

*Apr 1* "Jack George went up river to set beaver traps."

Skook's Landing. East of Fireside, there was a road that went from the Alaska Highway to Skook's Landing on the north bank of the Liard at its junction with the Kechika. Crossing the Liard to the Kechika was hazardous, for the river's current was strong and downstream there were rapids. Windrem Family collection

*Apr 10* "Louis Boya, Charlie Porter and Emma Alec all came up from Porter Lake. They say too much water on the ice now."

*Apr 11* "I got all the supplies for this bunch. Louis Boya, Charley Porter and Emma Alec left at noon for Porter Lake on the Turnagain River close to the junction of the Kechika."

*Apr 13* "The Indians bought some grub for the return trip up river."

*Apr 14* "Jack and Frank George and Allan Charlie left for their beaver hunt up the Frog River."

*Apr 15* "I destroyed the ice plane landing, marked a landing on the gravel bar."

During the first part of May, Freer spent a few days checking all the horses before leaving for the summer.

*May 13* "I got in all my horses today."

*May 14* "I saw all the horses, two still missing."

*May 16* "I hunted horses all day."

*May 17* "I hunted horses all day, finally found the government horses."

*May 18* "I took the government horses and rigging up to Skook's. Skook was pretty glum. Mabel Frank was there and Frank George. Alan Charlie, Jack George and Ernie Frank up at City Cabins looking for horses."

Five days later, Freer prepared to work for Hu Gabrielse again.

*May 23* "I got everything ready to go out. Gabrielse sent a kicker in to bring the boat down with. The Beaver plane came in and went on to Skook's. Buck Adsit came in too."

*May 25* "Frank George, Alan Charlie, Buck Adsit and I went to City Cabins. I forded the Gataga River, very easy, took the broken motor out of the boat and left it."

*May 26* "We shoved the boat into the river and made as far as Turnagain River. The river is sure damn low. Sure lots of bars. Stopped at Skook's, at Dust Cabin and Horn Creek. The 18 horse Evinrude motor sure handles the boat nice."

### May 27–September 11 Work for Geological Survey of Canada as packer and boatman

On May 27, the men travelled down to the junction of the Kechika and Liard Rivers, where they pulled the boat out. Gabrielse was doing most of his geological mapping in the Kechika valley during the 1960 field season and he intended to use Freer's riverboat for much of his transportation. Unfortunately, Freer's boat and motor did not prove to be reliable.

> *May 28* "Buck Adsit and I pulled the boat out of the river to be overhauled."

For several reasons, Freer spent the first week of June waiting around camp before he and Adsit began repairing the boat.

> *June 11* "We worked on the boat all day, a very slow job. H. Gabrielse was down."

On June 14, Gabrielse returned to check on the progress of the boat repairs.

> *June 15* "Gabrielse was up twice from mile 508. He took Buck Adsit down for a few days."

It rained almost every day during the next week.

> *June 23* "H. Gabrielse was up from his camp at 508 and says they are isolated as water all around their camp."

In mid-July, Freer wrote:

> *July 12* "Stu [Blusson], senior assistant from Gabrielse camp at mile 508, went to Watson Lake at 6 PM and returned at 12:30 AM. Gabrielse was with Stu on return. Gabrielse had to take his son to Cassiar for an operation and son and mother, Mrs. Gabrielse, are in Whitehorse now. We worked on the boat." (Gabrielse's son had an emergency appendectomy at the Whitehorse hospital.)

> *July 14* "Buck Adsit was up to the telephone office and the 109 hp grey marine engine was ordered. He also got the fiberglass paint $55.75. We worked on the boat. Art Swannell from Victoria was in and we went to Fireside and had a couple of beer. Art is doing survey work along the highway."

By July 18, the repairs to the boat were finished and Freer was waiting for a new engine to arrive. On July 24, Freer heard that the boat motor had been shipped from Vancouver on July 15. While he was waiting for the motor to arrive, Freer worked at Fireside.

> *Aug 2* "Gabrielse's party went up to the boat camp today from mile 508. They will be going up river in about a week."

> *Aug 4* "Still no engine, and working at Fireside. Gabrielse was up today to see me. He is getting quite anxious."

On August 5, the motor finally arrived. Three days later, the repairs were completed and Freer took a trial run. After two months, Freer's riverboat was finally ready.

On August 9, Freer and Gabrielse's crew began taking gasoline up the Kechika River. By August 14, Gabrielse made camp at the mouth of the Turnagain River.

> *Aug 16* "Gabrielse came in with Al and a super cub and is flying out of here. Went to the mouth of the Muddy to pick up the Swannell party to survey land up at my place and Skook's."

To add to a stressful situation for Freer, BC land surveyor Art Swannell arrived. He was doing some government surveys in the area and had been instructed to survey the land that Freer, Skook, and Dowsette wanted to purchase. Five years after the papers had been filed, the three men were getting their properties surveyed. It was late in the field season, and both Swannell's and Gabrielse's crews were behind schedule because of Freer's misadventures, so he was busy trying to keep them working efficiently.

Freer had some hectic days transporting Gabrielse's and Swannell's crews. Gabrielse had been unable to do much geological mapping, so he wanted to maximize the remaining time. Freer started transporting Swannell's crew to the pre-emption that he needed to have surveyed.

> *Aug 19* "We stopped for lunch at the GSC [Geological Survey of Canada] camp, Gabrielse's for coffee, picked up gas and went on to the Horn Creek of mine. Broke the steering cable."

> *Aug 20* "Showed Art Swannell my stake and triangulation post, returned to the Turnagain and the GSC camp."

The next day, Willard moved Gabrielse's camp to the mouth of Matulka Creek near Skook's ranch. From August 22 to 25, Freer transported both Swannell's and Gabrielse's crews, since they were working along the Kechika

River in the same area. On August 26, Freer went to Horneline Creek and picked up the Swannell survey party. He dropped them off at Cottonwood Flats to survey a lot there for Skook. Freer stayed with Swannell's crew for the night on August 27. The next day he returned to Gabrielse's camp. The last three days of the month were cold and rainy.

> *Sept 1* "Art Swannell was up from his camp and returned. Gabe and Swannell went to Skook's with the helicopter, but Skook not home." The next day, Freer took Swannell and his crew to Skook's place, then returned to the Geological Survey of Canada crew.

> *Sept 6* Freer went to the Turnagain River. "We are moving out now. The strut bearing support went out. Repaired it." The next day Freer left the Turnagain camp with Gabrielse's crew and went to the boat landing near the junction of the Kechika and the Liard Rivers.

> *Sept 7* "Gabrielse and 3 of the crew went to Watson Lake. Tore a hole in the boat."

> *Sept 8* "The boys helped me to haul the boat out of the water for repairs." For the following two days, Freer worked on the boat.

## September 11–December 31 Fireside and Alaska Highway

> *Sept 11* "Gabrielse and party left for Watson Lake today. The job is finished now and all the boys are going out."

> *Sept 13* "Gabrielse and Bill Loblaw [the cook] went south today. They are finished for the season."

Freer resumed working on the boat.

> *Sept 15* "I went up to Fireside and got my strut and bearing for the boat, worked on the boat." When he put the boat in the water the next day, he found that it was leaking.

> *Sept 17* "I tried out the boat and it nearly sank on me so I shall have to give up the idea. Pulled the boat out and went to Fireside for the night. Hauled all my stuff up to Fireside and stored it away until next spring." Freer's riverboat had not been a successful or reliable means of transportation for Gabrielse and his crew.

Freer flew from Watson Lake to Skook's place to see Art Swannell.

*Sept 23* "Art Swannell and 3 of the boys started for Lower Post September 18. They got tired of waiting for me and thought possibly I was wrecked as so long overdue.... Two of Swannell's party still working."

*Sept 25* "The plane arrived today and we went to Watson Lake. Art Swannell arrived today too, by trail. Picked up 2 of the boys at 66 mile, one with a cut knee."

*Sept 27* "I left Watson Lake with Swannell's party. I stayed at Fireside. Started to work at noon. Swannell's party left."

Freer's delay in getting Gabrielse's geological mapping started also impacted Art Swannell's surveying in the Kechika. However, Gabrielse did manage to complete the geological mapping he had scheduled for the summer, and Swannell surveyed Freer's pre-emption.

Freer spent the first half of October doing carpentry jobs and pumping gas. From October 21 to 25, it snowed every day. The wet, heavy snow made driving difficult. At the end of the month, there was "a big Halloween party and sure some funny costumes."

November was an uneventful month at Fireside. On the first day of December, "Ken Windrem left for Dawson Creek with the truck for a new light plant." He returned nine days later. By December 18, Windrem had the new power plant running.

# 1961

Freer's three-ring binder covers the years from 1958 to 1961. The last week of 1960 and the first nine months of 1961 are missing. Hu Gabrielse's field books show that he spent the summer of 1961 continuing and completing his geological mapping of northern BC in the Rabbit River drainage. Freer is listed as a member of Gabrielse's crew, and the work went much more efficiently. In 1962, Gabrielse began geological mapping of the western portion of the Northwest Territories and spent the rest of his career in the two northern territories.

## October 1–December 31 Fireside and the Alaska Highway

When Freer's diary resumed on October 1, 1961, he was back at Fireside at a busy time. During the second week of the month, it snowed several days and vehicles slid off the road, keeping the wrecker busy.

*Oct 11* The "Alaska transport had the road blocked for 14 hours at Mile 488."

During the last half of the month, there was less traffic on the Alaska Highway, and there were no major events. November was a quiet month, but it snowed several times. At the end of the month, the temperature dropped below –40°C for a few nights.

Ken Windrem returned on December 1.

*Dec 18* "Margo went to Watson Lake and returned with Ken's son, Dale, from Vancouver. She nearly froze in the car. George Nelms and wife left for a month's holiday. They are flying out from Watson."

*Dec 19* "We were fairly busy here. A chartered bus is taking a load of men out from Cassiar asbestos. One recovery south at mile 517."

*Dec 25* Freer described Christmas Day. "A fairly quiet day here today. Had 5 Herda drivers here that are broke down. They are enjoying themselves as much as could be. Roy had a recovery to Coal River at Mile 533. Cloudy and cold."

*Dec 31* "Everybody went to the party. There were plenty of drunks around tonight. Jim Neville and Mary had a fight. Jensen passed out. The DP from Fireside passed out early and had to be put to bed. It was quite a good party."

## FIRESIDE—THE COMMUNITY

Mile 543—Fireside was the site of one of the original camps built along the Alaska Highway during its construction. It was located along the north bank of the Liard River near the junction with the Kechika River. Fireside received its name from the large stone fireplace in the lodge that was built there in the 1940s. With a population of about fifty people, it was one of the larger communities along this section of the highway during the 1960s and 1970s.

The 1959 Canadian Government Travel Bureau guide described the services available at Fireside: "Accom[modation], housekeeping cabins, gas & oil, repairs, wrecker service, trailer space with electricity." The inn could handle twenty-eight people, and telephone service was available. The Highway Department established a maintenance camp at Fireside for this section of the Alaska Highway and Canadian National Telegraph (which had the telephone network that had been installed along the Alaska Highway) had a repeater station there.

In the late 1950s, a post office was established at the lodge and the community became officially called Fireside. A Quonset hut used during the Alaska Highway construction served as the community curling rink, and there was a small but well-equipped recreation centre where movies were shown.

The Alaska Highway started to become a tourist and adventure destination in the 1950s. The road was gravel and rough in many places, and travel was slow. Flat tires, mechanical breakdowns and accidents were common occurrences. There were many lodges and camps established along the highway, and these businesses needed employees. Since there was only a small local population, most of the workers at the tourist sites along the highway came from other locations or were hired as they travelled along the highway. This created a transient work force, and the Alaska Highway lodges and camps often operated without sufficient employees. Fireside was representative of the lodges along the Alaska Highway.

In 1968, Nanaimo Bulldozing won the contract for this section of the highway and they built housing for families at Fireside at the Fireside compound. In the late 1960s and early 1970s, the community had sufficient children to have a one-room school for a few years.

Margo used this postcard to advertise Fireside Lodge. Nelms Family collection

A helicopter view of the Alaska Highway going through the community of Fireside. This photo was taken in the early 1960s before the expansion of the lodge and its outbuildings. Windrem Family collection

Fireside in the winter. Windrem Family collection

The Alaska Highway and the buildings on the south side between the highway and the Liard River. This photo shows the lodging built around Fireside Inn in the 1960s. The lodge is in the centre of the picture. The sleeping cabins are on the right in the foreground. The vehicles are around the gas and car repair stations in the centre. Windrem Family collection

Loiselle was one of the main trucking companies on the Alaska Highway in the 1960s. Windrem Family collection

Going out on a recovery. Ken received most of the calls for service for truck vehicles that needed to be recovered. He had both the skills and equipment to do this. Windrem Family collection

## 1962

### January 1–March 8 Fireside, Alaska Highway

During the 1960s, helicopters and airplanes displaced horses as the main means of transporting people and supplies to the remote areas of northern BC. The four summers of packing and using his riverboat for the Geological Survey of Canada was Freer's next-to-last major project. Freer started spending more time at Fireside on the Alaska Highway, and it became his main source of employment income. However, he still retained his cabin along the Kechika, and in his diary, he always called it home. With a riverboat, it only took one or two days to travel upstream to his cabin (depending on the strength of the current), and less than a day to come downstream. Freer kept his herd of horses, and he almost always came to his place in the late winter to check on them.

A car repair at the beginning of 1962 illustrates the challenges faced when repairing vehicles at the car shops along the Alaska Highway.

> *Jan 2* "Roy [Osborne, the mechanic] had a recovery from mile 582. It is a 62 Plymouth, the axle went." A transmission was taken out of a car in Portland, Oregon, and sent by air to

Watson Lake, arriving four days later. Unfortunately, it was the wrong transmission.

*Jan 7* The mechanic and a helper "took the transmission up to Watson Lake to a lathe and got it ground down. They returned in the evening and put everything together."

January was a cold and snowy month.

*Jan 17* "All the Army fuel lines are froze up today. The government have summer fuel."

The popular curling bonspiels started during the last weekend in January.

*Jan 28* "Coal River curling bonspiel ended late this evening. Everybody seems to have had a very good time they say. They all went home happy anyway. Still snowing too and the plows are out steady."

*Jan 30* "Lots of trucks on the road hauling oil rigs in to Smith River and Dawson city."

The Cassiar bonspiel started on February 1. The next weekend, there was a big curling bonspiel at Watson Lake.

Freer wrote about some of his work during February.

*Feb 14* "Getting quite a lot of work done on new dining room. Got the window frames in now and ready for the glass as soon as [it] warms up some." A couple of times he took ice off the roof, and one day he worked in the café.

Freer intended to fly to the Kechika at the end of February, but inclement weather prevented this until March 8. One day, while he was waiting, Freer and two other men got paid for four hours of work loading a large van for Canada Tungsten.

## March 8–May 3 Kechika River Valley

*Mar 8* "I finally got a plane out to my place at Dust cabin."

The rest of his supplies arrived the next day. Freer spent most of March checking on his horses and feeding the ones that were thin.

*Apr 18* "I was down to feed my horses again today.… Jack George and Ernie Frank were down for the night. They are on the beaver hunt now."

*Apr 19* "I was down to the horses again today with their oats."

*May 3–December 31 Alaska Highway*

Near the end of the month, the river opened up.

> *Apr 29* "I went to Skook's, arrived there at 8 PM."

Freer stayed at the ranch until May 3, when a plane came to take him to Watson Lake. Two days later he went to Fireside.

> *May 7* "Went down to see the boat, but could not drive down as too much snow on the road. The boat is okay."

On May 16, Margo's dad arrived on the bus to stay for the summer and help around the lodge.

> *May 20* "I went down to my boat, it is still okay. River is rising very slow."

Freer spent the following days putting shingles on several buildings. By the latter part of the month, the lodge became busy almost every day. On June 4, he and Margo's father started to put shingles on two more cabins.

Ken and Margo began a new activity that summer—a hamburger stand at Liard Hot Springs.

> *June 6* "We started to build a trailer house for a hamburger stand."

> *June 7* "I helped Margo's dad to build the trailer house. It is slow work."

> *June 26* "Ken moved the hamburger stand to mile 497 at the Liard hot springs."

During July, everyone working at Fireside was busy. Freer noted that Ken went to the hamburger and hot dog stand every day.

> *July 21* "The old man and I are in the construction business again. Hauled in a broken down truck yesterday."

> *July 31* "The rooms are full nearly every night."

> *Aug 6* On BC Day weekend, "Two large trucks broke down here Saturday and of course can't order parts until Tuesday."

> *Aug 13* "We were sure real busy all day with everything, all our rooms stayed full all day. Some of the people went fishing and caught plenty and some picked a lot of raspberries."

Near the end of August, a tragedy occurred at Fireside.

> *Aug 28* Three days before he was scheduled to finish his

summer job, leave Fireside, and begin his first year at university, "Percy Nelms was killed in a cave-in in a waterline ditch. Flew a doctor down from Watson Lake and the police were also down along with many officials."

*Aug 29* "The Nelms left for Fort St. John for the funeral of their son. An inquest was held and Margot and Ken left after the inquest for the funeral. I was on the inquest. They found the cause of death was accidental."

Female friends seldom appear in Freer's diaries, but in late August, he wrote about one.

*Aug 31* "We were quite busy all day with everything. Mary Cherry and I are working together. We went for a drive down to the whirlpool as she had never seen it before. She is a mighty fine woman, not stuck up and very nice to talk to. She likes the same things as I do, that is the outside or out of doors."

*Sept 2* "Mary Cherry and I went down to the whirlpool campsite for a while and looked around."

Freer and Cherry spent time together after work on the next weekend.

*Sept 8* "Mary Cherry and I went to the whirlpool and Smith River Falls."

*Sept 9* "Mary and I went to the head of whirlpool and looked around. She took lots of pictures."

*Sept 10* This day marked the end of summer at Fireside for several people. "Margo's dad and [her] son's wife left for their respective homes in Edmonton and in Nanaimo. Mary Cherry left also to go by Edmonton to her place at Nelson BC where she works. Very quiet now around here."

In mid-September, the road surfacing crew worked around Fireside.

*Sept 15* "The whole surface crew came in late tonight and spent the evening. Nobody was feeling any pains. Margo left for Fort St. John and expects to be away for about a week."

On September 24 and 27, Freer recorded that the surface crew was hauling gravel for new houses across the road.

October was an uneventful month except for one tragedy.

*Oct 20* "A Thunderbird car collided with an Allied Van Lines at mile 608 and a woman was killed. The man and kid were sent to the hospital. Car demolished."

*Nov 8* "7 CNT boarders and roomers here now. We are full house nearly every night. The gas sales are quite good every day too."

On the evening of November 13, Margo left by car for Victoria.

*Nov 14* "Margo broke down at Summit and hitched a ride to Fort Nelson. Ken has gone down with the truck and Plymouth loaded to pick up Margo."

*Nov 16* "Ken arrived back late with the wrecked car. It was sure badly damaged."

For Christmas, Freer hosted the Nelms for dinner.

*Dec 29* "We had a New Year's party tonight at the Army road camp. Everybody had a very good time." The next day, several people went to the New Year's dance at Watson Lake.

# 1963

*January 1–March 7 Alaska Highway*

There was not much newsworthy at Fireside in January except for one entry.

*Jan 26* "The police were down yesterday to pick up Amy Frank $100 fine or a year in jail. Leroux and McDonald paid the fine and then they all went on a big drunk."

In late January and early February, there were again vehicles at Fireside that took several days to repair.

*Jan 28* "Ken pulled in a car with a broken axle. They are in room 11. Four children. They will be here for several days until new parts come from Dawson Creek. There was another car with no heater and four small children and broke heading for Portland."

On February 4, a transmission arrived for a '63 Chevy and the vehicle got repaired.

*Feb 5* "The Chevy 63 car got away this a.m. after being here for 14 days."

On February 9 and 10, there was a curling bonspiel at Watson Lake. There was a death among the highway crew personnel in late February.

*Feb 20* "Ed Erickson, heavy duty operator for the road camp, had a stroke and died between Lower Post and Watson Lake."

*Feb 26* "Ed Erickson's funeral today at Watson Lake and there sure was a very large crowd. Everybody went from here. Four cars went up loaded and returned late."

### March 7–June 2 Kechika River valley

On March 7, Freer went to Watson Lake.

*Mar 8* "I flew home to the Muddy at Dust cabin. Saw some wolves at a kill on the river."

*Mar 9* "A squirrel got into my cache and sure made a mess of things."

*Mar 10* "I looked up my horses today and they are in very good shape. They were sure glad to see me. I fooled around with them most of the day."

*Mar 26* "I saw my horses and finally got bells on them. They are sure looking good."

Freer spent April working around his cabin. On April 26, he went to visit Skook and returned on April 29.

*May 13* Freer went to the Diamond J Ranch. "I had quite a load of magazines for Skook. I cut trail on the way up." Freer spent a day helping Skook get his garden ready and doing odds and ends. He returned to his cabin on May 15.

Freer had some final transactions for fur in May.

*May 16* "Bill Allen and Charley Porter were up from Starvation and got some grub. They are trapping beaver down there."

*May 22* "Charley Porter, Kenny Porter and Bill Allen were up from Fish Creek and got some grub. They brought up some beaver. They returned down river."

Near the end of May, Freer made a raft and used it to return to Fireside.

*May 31* "Camped at the mouth of the Kechika River where it flows into the Liard River 1 mile above the boat landing and Whirlpool canyon. Sure had some wild rides today. Lots of rough water.... There was just enough water behind the Lone Sister to allow to go that way."

Freer had to decide how he would cross the Liard the next day.

*June 1* "I scouted the Liard River up from the mouth of the Kechika and shall take my raft up and cross to the north side and down to the boat landing. I cut my raft down in size to 3 logs as the 5 logs would take me too long to cross over."

*June 2* "I lined the raft and all my stuff up the Liard and crossed over in good shape. I went down to the boat landing and stayed for the night at the landing." The next day, he began working at Fireside.

## *June 2–December 31 Alaska Highway and boat trips up Kechika River*

It was the summer tourist season along the Alaska Highway, and Freer's diary entries indicated that the Fireside Inn was busy almost every day, and its rooms were fully occupied almost every evening. In early July, some painters came to paint signs for the lodge. "The Army are putting a new road across from the lodge to the main road."

During the second week in July, it rained for a few days. The *Whitehorse Daily Star* ran a front-page headline in bold on July 11 that stated "Alaska Highway Washouts Close Route To All Traffic."

*July 10* "The road was closed in the Muncho Lake area and south as 42 washouts. We are sure filled to the hilt. Every space is chock full. Rained quite heavy here today and no let up."

*July 11* "The road crew are all working on the washed out road. We have a very good bunch here, all anxious to go but not troublesome."

*July 12* The road "opened today to one-way traffic and everybody left. I was quite busy at the pumps."

During the second half of July, Freer and George Nelms travelled up the Kechika River.

*July 18* "George Nelms and I went up river a ways with his boat. It sure does travel." Three days later, the two men travelled about thirty kilometres up the Muddy.

*July 21* "We were above all the rough water, took up 30 gallons of gas. Saw one black bear swimming the Liard."

The next week, Freer, George Miller and George Nelms departed in the early evening of July 25 and camped about sixteen kilometres up the Kechika River.

*July 27* The men "dumped everything at my place and went up to Skook's and returned to Dust cabin." A six-hour and forty-minute trip the next day brought them back to the boat landing on the north side of the Liard. Some of that time was spent fishing.

In August, Freer and Margo's father worked on improving the foundation walls of the lodge by digging out some of the walls and pouring cement into some places. Freer made several entries in his diary regarding the work the two men did. By August 30, the men had finished pouring cement for the summer.

*Sept 2* Margo's father left for Edmonton. "He sure is not well at all," Freer wrote.

*Sept 6* Freer met Hu Gabrielse who "came out from Canada Tungsten in the Northwest Territories on the head of the Hyland River. He says snow in there now."

Freer and George Miller took a hunting trip by boat, departing from Fireside on September 11. They hunted unsuccessfully for goats for three days, but Miller shot a large bull moose. By September 25, they returned to Fireside.

*Oct 7* "We have 12 CNT men boarding here now and more to come."

*Oct 8* "We were quite busy here all day, quite a few people travelling and a bunch of CNT moved in to build a new repeater office." On October 10, Freer noted that the CNT crew were at Fireside and the rooms were full.

*Oct 16* "The crew of CNT are still here and a pole crew at mile 578."

*Oct 31* Freer described Halloween. "Some of the crew were in and kind of laid one on. The Halloween pranksters were out."

*Nov 2* "Ken and Margo went to the masquerade dance at Muncho Lake. There are a lot of people travelling. Snow is quite slippery." They returned the next day.

*Nov 6* Freer described a busy day: "3 Hill and Hill trucks in and fuelled up. One over the bank at mile 586. Travelite cat and truck came down and got truck out. Travelite tractor broke a brownie. Hill and Hill truck arrived late from over the bank. Ken pulled in a car from 558 and got him on his way. Another car with trouble. All the rooms are full."

Freer wrote that Christmas was a quiet day.

*Dec 25* "Ken and Margo went to Nelms for Christmas dinner. Rose and I had a very quiet dinner. A party came in at the hall all the sudden and a very good time was had by everyone. It broke up at 4 AM. Snowed some last night."

# 1964

### *January 1–March 28 Fireside*

Freer spent the winter of 1964 at Fireside again. By now, he was familiar with the routine of winter along the Alaska Highway. Some days were busy, while most were quiet. Weather and road conditions were important factors in the ebb and flow of people and traffic.

There was a community New Year's Eve party at the recreation hall that lasted until 5 a.m. Freer had the Nelms over for New Year's dinner. Curling started in January.

*Jan 6* "We finally got started to curl for the first time. Had a very good game."

Since Freer was at Fireside, Ken and Margo left for a month of vacation. At the end of January, Fireside hosted a curling bonspiel.

*Feb 1* "We were very busy here all day with everything. The curling is going on as scheduled and everybody is having a wonderful time. The place here is chock full and CNT road camp houses are all full from people of Watson Lake and Muncho Lake.... We are feeding most of the people at the café." The curling bonspiel finished on Sunday in the late afternoon.

*Feb 6* "George and Mrs. Nelms went to Watson Lake to pick up their daughter coming in on the plane and returned."

*Feb 10* "Mrs. Nelms was over to do post office report." Margo was the mistress for the post office, and while she was on vacation, Mrs. Nelms handled the position.

On February 12, Freer noted that he had shovelled snow and ice all day because the lodge roof was leaking. There was a picture show at the Rec Hall that evening. On the weekends during February, there were bonspiels at nearby communities. The bonspiels finished in the first week of March with one at Muncho Lake, but the residents of Fireside continued to curl at their own rink during the first half of March. Margo and Ken returned from their vacation.

*Mar 16* "Ken went to Mile 505 to pick up a car collision. Some people hurt bad. Ken took both vehicles to the Liard Lodge Mile 496. The ambulance took all the people to Fort Nelson."

*Mar 18* "Margo went to Watson Lake and hit a car at Mile 610. The other car $600 damages and plenty to Margo's car."

## March 28–June 8 Kechika River valley

Freer flew back to his place on the Kechika on March 28.

*Mar 28* "Got things straightened out and went to the meadow and saw the horses. They were sure glad to see me and are in very good shape. The horses have been in and out all winter by the signs. All the dishes are left dirty and frozen, water and some of the pots."

*Mar 29* Freer noted that there was a lot of stuff missing out of the cache and that "all the stuff I brought up last summer was gone through. The horses came in and bummed me for some oats."

*Mar 30* "The horses are in and still bumming for oats. They are sure in good shape."

*Apr 2* Stan Bridcut came with a load of goods for Freer. "He had a passenger who drives bus between Watson Lake and Cassiar and now has Amos Alec's hunting area near Turnagain River." Bridcut brought Freer's remaining goods on April 7.

Once again, Freer was actively involved in the spring fur trade in the Kechika River valley. These are three of several entries.

*Apr 12* "Jack George and Ernie Frank came down from up river with a wolf and four Beaver, all Green hides. They stayed here for supper and stayed at Frank George's cabin a couple hundred yards from here."

*Apr 13* "Jack George, Ernie Frank and Perry Frank went down river looking for beaver. They expect to be gone for several days. Louis Boya and Frank George came down from up river and are heading down river. They stayed at the cabin here. I stretched 5 beaver for Jack and Ernie here."

*Apr 14* "Jack George, Ernie Frank and Perry Frank went back up river. They left one beaver."

Freer had some diary entries describing the wildlife he observed.

*Apr 22* "The ice opened here and there is a channel through. Four caribou swam the river and went west. A moose swam and went east. Saw two deer on the hill." Two days later, he noted that there were lots of cranes going north, and on April 29 he recorded that about ten flocks of swans and sandhill cranes flew over.

Freer went to Skook's place on May 7, cutting trail along the way. He stayed overnight and returned to his cabin the next day.

*May 10* "Louis Boya, Jack George and Perry Frank came down river on a raft. They camped here overnight."

*May 16* "Louis Boya and Frank George came down from up river. They camped here overnight."

*May 17* "I stretched seven beaver for Jack George and five more to fix up. Louis and Frank went down river at noon. Jack and Perry came in with a raft from up river. They had a beaver. They got some grub and continued on down river."

*May 27* "Jack and Frank George, Louis Boya and Perry Frank returned from their beaver hunt. They did alright."

*May 28* The "Indians are busy stretching beaver. They have over 30 stretched here."

*May 29* "Jack, Frank, Louis and Perry left for their cabin up river.... All the Indians returned back up river and camped at Trail Creek."

*June 8* Freer came down the river with two men from Fort St. John who were on a fishing trip. "We left my place at 8:15, stopped at Turnagain River and arrived boat landing at 4 PM. We were five hours and 10 minutes. Kechika and Liard rivers are bank full."

### June 8–July 3 Alaska Highway

Freer went to work at Fireside for a few weeks, for the lodge was busy. On July 3, Freer, George Nelms and Jim Neville left for Dust Cabin, arriving the next day.

### July 3–27 Preparing for hunting trips

Nelms and Neville returned to Fireside on Sunday, July 5 while Freer remained at Dust Cabin.

*July 10* "Dalziel brought Douglas Reid over from Dease Lake at 9 PM to help me go to Sandpile Lakes later on."

Freer was going to spend part of the summer working for Robin Dalziel on hunting trips. In mid-July, Freer worked with the horses in preparation for the hunting. He had everything ready by July 23.

### July 27–September 6 Packer and hunting guide for Robin Dalziel

On July 27, Freer started working for Robin Dalziel. After two days of travelling the men arrived at Sandpile Lake and Dalziel's camp. Freer's main job was to pack and move camp for the hunters and look after the horses. He cleared trail where necessary, and sometimes took a hunter for a day. Dalziel's hunting area was west of the Kechika River.

On August 18, Freer took two hunters and got a sheep and goats. Freer and the hunters started travelling to Sandpile Lakes on August 23, arriving the next day. The men hunted and fished around the lakes for the next two days. Freer recorded the group's activities during the end of August and through the first week of September.

### September 6–14 Travel to cabin

By September 6, Freer's work with Robin Dalziel was finished, and he returned to his cabin on September 14.

### September 14–27 Worked on fencing and clearing trails

### September 28–October 5 Raft trip to Fireside

On September 28, Freer started down the Kechika River by raft, heading for Fireside. It was a leisurely trip, and he reached the mouth of the river on October 4.

> *Oct 4* "I ran all the rough water including the Lone Sister. The river is very low and some of the riffles are sort of treacherous as the rocks are close to the surface."

> *Oct 5* "I made a raft and crossed the Liard River in very good shape.... I walked up to Fireside in late evening."

### October 5–17 Work at Fireside and trip back to Kechika

Freer worked at Fireside for a week. On October 17, he flew with Stan Bridcut back to his cabin.

### October 18–December 31 Kechika River valley

At the end of October, there were some airplane flights into the Kechika.

> *Oct 25* "BC Yukon Air Service Beaver brought in Jack and Frank George and Ernest Abou and their dogs."

> *Oct 26* The Beaver transported "Louis Boya, daughter and small boy, Bill Allen and wife and baby and Don McCook's son who has been out with Del Monica on the upper Dease river hunting. Jack George went out as his sore arm is bothering him."

> *Oct 28* "The BC Yukon air service piper cub circled here and landed downriver with Jack George and returned to Watson Lake with young Emil McCook of Fort Ware."

Freer had visitors in the second half of November.

> *Nov 15* "Bill and Louis went to Horn Creek and looked after their traps.... Ann and Bill [Allen] were over in the evening to listen to the radio." Two days later they also came over in the evening.

> *Nov 18* "Jack George and Ernest Abou got some groceries and returned up river. Louis was out hunting, Bill working on the fence."

> *Nov 19* "Bill, Louis and I worked on the Dust Creek pasture fence. My cat followed me in the morning to the fence and I had to go get her this afternoon."

Freer went to the Diamond J on November 23 and stayed two nights.

> *Nov 24* "Skook and I played cribbage and nothing else but

the usual chores. Jack and Ernest went down to Davie and up the creek to look after traps there. They got a lynx at the lake."

The next day Freer returned to his cabin. On November 26, Louis and Bill got a lynx and beaver. Louis and Bill came over and made some snares the next day. On November 30, Louis and Bill went to Horneline Creek to check on their traps.

The weather turned cold in mid-December, and the temperature dropped to below –40°C on several evenings. Freer spent a lot of time cutting and packing wood. The cold weather limited activity, but Louis shot a moose on Christmas day.

# 1965

*January 1–June 18 Kechika River valley*

In early January the temperature was cold; from January 4 to January 7, it got below –40°C every night. Freer spent much of his time cutting and packing wood. Almost every day Louis Boya came over from his cabin to visit. Bob Harrison flew in with a load of supplies.

> *Jan 1* "Louis and Bill were over, and Bill and Ann were over in the evening and played cards."

> *Jan 5* "I received all my mail and I got cake and candy from Mrs. Nelms."

Harrison went back to Watson Lake with Ann and Bill Allen and their two children. Ann was pregnant and not feeling well. On January 10, the weather started to moderate.

January 13 marked the beginning of an event that received national coverage in Canadian newspapers and even in some American ones.

> *Jan 13* "Joe Hayes and wife Emma and one child, a baby, arrived here from Amos Alec's trapline on the Turnagain River above the forks of Mosquito Creek. They lost two children on way over, starvation, no grub. It is about 40 miles [64 kilometres] to Amos Alec's."

Freer was able to supply food, but his radio was not working, so he could not call for assistance. Joe Hayes and his family stayed with Louis Boya and his family. Freer has several diary entries about the incident.

> *Jan 14* "Joe Hayes was over."

> *Jan 15* "Joe Hayes was over and got some more grub."

*Jan 16* "Waited for a plane, tried to flag BC Yukon Piper down but apparently the pilot was sleeping. Louis and Frank had a large fire on the river bar. I marked SOS on ice and had orange flag but no dice. The 2 dead children are 5 and 3 years old."

Hayes needed to get assistance and more food, so he travelled to Skook's ranch.

*Jan 17* "Joe Hayes left for Skook's at 9:30 AM. BC Yukon Piper Cub went to Skook's and returned to Watson Lake. I finally woke the pilot up. He saw us today as he swung over to us but never landed, went on to Watson Lake. Frank George was over today and bought some groceries."

*Jan 18* "BC Yukon piper cub went to Skook's with oats and returned to here with Joe (Lucky) Hayes. BC Yukon Beaver came in with the police, [picked up] Joe and Emma Hayes and took them to Watson Lake. The plane will be in again tomorrow to pick up the 2 dead children left on the trail through by Moodie Lakes on the route to the Turnagain River. Frank and Louis were up after the planes left."

*Jan 19* "BC Yukon piper cub brought John Johnny in to help Louis Boya to look for the 2 dead children between here and Turnagain River. A plane went on to Skook's and returned to Watson."

*Jan 20* "Louis Boya and John Johnny went up to Moodie Lakes trail to the Turnagain River and picked up the 2 dead bodies and put them in my cache here. They left here at 10:30 AM and arrived back at 7 PM."

*Jan 22* "BC Yukon air service piper cub was in and picked up the 2 dead children and John Johnny to Watson Lake. And also a Cessna 180 went to Skook's with Jack George and returned to Watson Lake."

# JOE "LUCKY" HAYES

*British Colonist*, January 20, 1965, p. 3. "Heroic trek in vain: sick children die on trail"

Around January 20, 1965, almost every daily newspaper in Canada (and several in the United States) published an article similar to this one that provided extensive detail of the tragic event. This article comes from the *British Colonist*, and is accessible on the "British Colonist 1858–1980" website. Louis Boya, who had a prominent role in this incident, was also involved in 1963 in the dramatic rescue of Ralph Flores and Helen Kishen. They were in a plane crash in the same region of northern BC and survived for forty-nine days before being located.

> A desperate 60 mile-trek [96 kilometre] through a wilderness mountain pass failed last week to save the lives of 2 young children who became ill at a remote northern British Columbia camp site.
>
> George Alex, 5, and his stepsister, Gloria Hayes, 15 months, died on the trail as their parents, Joseph (Lucky) Hayes, 24, and his wife Emma, 23, attempted to carry them to a ranch where medical aid could be summoned by radio. Their food supplies had also run short.
>
> Nature of the illness was not disclosed.
>
> A third child, a 6 month old boy, survived the trip, made in 30 below zero [−22°C] weather. The parents walked on snowshoes. Two packed dogs carried meager food supplies, utensils and a sleeping bag.
>
> Mr. Hayes suffered a frozen foot. He was released after treatment at a nursing station in Watson Lake, a community near the BC-Yukon border, about 750 miles [1200 kilometres] northwest of Edmonton.
>
> Mr. and Mrs. Hayes and their infant son were flown to safety from a trapper's cabin on the Kechika River, 120 miles [192 kilometres] southwest of Watson Lake.
>
> **Bodies Cached**
>
> Two men left Tuesday for the Moodie Pass District to recover the bodies of the two children, cached in trees by the parents to ensure animals did not disturb the bodies.
>
> The Kechika River cabin is about 40 miles [64 kilometres] south of an area where Ralph Flores and Helen Kishen were plucked two years ago after surviving 49 days in the wilderness from a plane crash.

**Same Pilot**

Chuck Hamilton of Watson Lake, the pilot who rescued Miss Kishen and Flores, flew Mr. and Mrs. Hayes and the surviving child to Watson Lake from Louis Boya's cabin. [Louis Boya was also involved in 1963 in the dramatic rescue of Flores and Kishen.]

The Hayes family moved into the region from Lower Post, B.C. last October when Mr. Hayes was given a contract to supervise horses during the winter at Turnagain camp owned by Amos Alex, a big-game outfitter.

**60 Mile Hike**

RCMP said that when the eldest children became violently ill last week the couple decided to hike out to a ranch about 60 miles away.

Gloria died the afternoon of Tuesday, January 12, and George the following morning.

During the last week in January, Louis Boya was out checking his traps and he stopped several times at Freer's cabin.

> *Jan 26* "Jack George, Ernest Abou and Charlie Pete came down from up river."

The men stayed for two days, and on January 28, Ernest Abou bought some groceries.

> *Jan 29* "Stan Bridcut.... brought in a load for me. The manager from the Bank of commerce was in. I negotiated a $1000 loan from the bank. They returned to Watson. Jack George, Charlie Pete and Ernest Abou left for their trap line up river."

In February, Freer spent much of his time cutting and packing wood, and by February 15, he had his supply for the year. On February 7 and 8, Louis Boya came over in the evening to listen to the radio.

There was a lot of activity at Freer's cabin in March. Willard had several entries in his diary recording visits from the local inhabitants. Most of the time they were bringing fur to exchange for food. Louis Boya, Freer's closest neighbour, appears in several entries. Amos Alec and his family also came to Freer's cabin a few times. Ann and Bill Allen, along with Frank and Jack George, are among others mentioned.

Airplanes landed on snow-packed runways near Freer's place a few times during March. Louis Boya flew out to Watson Lake on March 4 and returned two weeks later. On the same March 18 flight, Freer sent out the fur that he had obtained in barter.

Trapping continued in April. Freer's diary has several entries describing the activities of the Indigenous people.

The weather continued to be cold and the snow was slow to melt, so beaver trapping extended into May. On May 26 Freer started cleaning up the yard and burning brush, while Louis and Bill were working on their beaver and Ann was helping them.

*May 28* "I bought Louis Boya's and Bill Allen's fur."

*May 30* "Amos Alec and his family came in from the Turnagain River with 3 horses. They say lots of ice on the lakes yet. He had 25 beaver."

The trapping finished in early June.

*June 2* Freer went to Dust Cabin. "Brought down seven beaver I bought off of Charlie Pete. Met Louis Boya at No. 6 going up river. They are all out after a few more beaver tonight."

Freer worked with his horses in early June, getting them ready for the summer.

*June 5* "I rented 5 head of horses to Eddie Miller."

*June 6* "Branded WF on 7 head of my horses that were here."

### June 18–July 24 Watson Lake and Canadian Geological Survey watchman, Mile 130, Cantung

Freer flew to Watson Lake on June 18 on Stan Bridcut's return flight from Amos Alec's place.

*June 22* "Went out with Hugh Gabrielse to the geological camp at Mile 130 Can-Tung Road…. The road is in very good condition. Stewart Blusson [Gabriele's assistant] was tackled by a grizzly, just received a scratch."

Once more, Freer had a connection with Cantung, and he was working for Hu Gabrielse again. Nine years previously, it took Freer about two weeks to pack into the mineral claim that Kennco had prospected for copper but which instead became western Canada's first tungsten mine. Now there was a road all the way to the site.

*June 23* "I am doing the cooking here and odds and ends for three men in the camp.... We are camped on a flight strip by Can-Tung road on the Highland River." On June 25, Freer noted that there had been lots of traffic on the road the previous couple of days.

*June 29* "Gabrielse and helicopter arrived at 2 PM across country from Lower Liard Mile 496 on Alaska Highway. They gassed up and had lunch here and left for Hay Hook Lake.... I am all alone here now."

The last part of June and early July were quiet at the camp.

*July 17* "I just wandered around here all day with absolutely nothing to do. I cut a stick of wood. No traffic on the road."

*July 23* "The road foreman for Can-Tung road and Ross River Road was in to look landing strip over. I cut my usual wood and wandered around. The large tanker went to the mine again today and the grader operators were in. The bus went to the mine and I went out to Watson Lake. I have finished this job."

## July 25–August 4 Preparing for work

Freer went to Fireside the next day.

*July 25* "I squared everything with George Nelms. I bought his boat, 27 foot long. He took me to the boat landing. I took off up river, picked up gas at the Moose licks that George had taken up before my kicker broke down at Red River. I sure have a load.... 8 hours to Red River."

On July 26, Freer cached his groceries, then floated down the Kechika to the Liard. The next day he arrived at Fireside and then got a ride to Watson Lake.

On July 28, Freer flew back to the Kechika and started preparing to work for Robin Dalziel again.

## August 4–September 14 Packer and hunting guide for Robin Dalziel

*Aug 4* Freer arrived at Deadwood Lake in the dark. "Amos and Margaret Alec here, everybody else is out on a hunt."

*Aug 5* "I packed up all the supplies and went through to my camp of last year on Mosquito Creek." The next day Freer arrived at the high-end camp he used last year and set up the tents.

*Aug 15* Freer arrived at the base camp at Deadwood Lake. From there he "took 2 hunters along with Dempsey [Alec] and rest of my horses" for ten days.

The hunters shot sheep and goats. Freer took other hunters through the first half of September and they were successful in getting goats and sheep. They also saw lots of wildlife.

*Sept 12* "Rained all day long with some snow. Robin's crew came in after dinner with no moose and really soaked too. They had fresh snow up high. One hunter lost his camera up there coming in. Cloudy and very wet. They are a disgruntled bunch of hunters."

## September 15–30 Return to cabin and errands

Freer started back to his cabin on September 15.

*Sept 20* "I had a very good horse wrangle and made home. Swam my horses and took one load over on a raft. The Kechika river is sure high from the heavy rains. The horses are glad to be home."

Freer spent a few days at his place. Then he flew with Bridcut to Watson Lake where he spent a few days before going to Fireside on September 28.

## September 30–October 29 Bring Gordon Toole's horses to Kechika River valley to winter

On the last day of September, Freer drove a horse truck about 300 kilometres to pick up Gordon Toole's horses. Freer had a job to winter Toole's horses in the Kechika valley.

*Oct 1* "Loaded Gordon Toole's horses and unloaded at radio range north of Watson Lake."

*Oct 12* Freer remained around Watson Lake until "Gordon Toole picked me up…. The horses are in tough condition. They have been kept shut up from feed too long. Gordon never found four head."

*Oct 14* "Swam the horses across the Liard and Dease rivers. Had to load some behind the boat to get them across. Leo Miller ran the boat. I picked up Mac Lutz to help to the home place." After laying over for a day, Freer started for home on October 16.

*Oct 29* "I had a good wrangle and left Moodie Creek and arrived home, rafted the Kechika River. Jack and Frank George, Ernie Frank and Ernest Abou came in today with Watson Lake Flying Service Beaver. The river is too deep for a ford."

### October 30–December 31 Kechika River valley

On November 8, Freer wrote that Toole's horses were filling out from the feed they were eating. In mid-November, Jack George, Ernie Frank and Ernest Abou came to his place to buy groceries and returned the next day.

*Nov 24* "BC Yukon air service piper cub came in and took Skook out to Watson Lake. Ernie Frank is looking after Skook's place while he is out. Skook is going to Fort St. John on a guide meeting."

December was a quiet month with a few visits from the Indigenous people who lived in Freer's area of the Kechika valley. On December 22, Frank George shot a moose and came to Freer's place. The next day Amos Alec and his family arrived. Amos and Frank packed in some meat, and Amos and Margaret came over for a visit. They also came over on Christmas. The weather turned cold after Christmas with temperatures below −40°C at night. Amos and Margaret came to visit almost every day.

## 1966

### January 1–July 2 Kechika River valley

The new year brought the continuation of cold weather, with most night temperatures falling below −40°C. Amos and Margaret came over with their children almost every evening. Freer spent a lot of time checking the horses to make sure that they were finding sufficient feed.

*Jan 7* "Amos made a stove out of a barrel and put up a tent to live in as Frank George is too damn cranky."

*Jan 10* "Amos and Margaret are staying in a tent and it is damn cold."

*Jan 13* It began to warm up. "I went with Amos and helped haul in a load of moose meat that he had shot yesterday. Frank George shot a moose today. I saw the Toole horses and they are looking very good. I cut a little wood and fed the lone horse in the South pasture."

On January 22 the temperature went back to –40°C and remained there until January 28. A couple of nights it went below –50°C.

*Jan 31* "I saw 3 of Toole's horses and 3 of mine. They are sure going downhill fast.... this has been 40 days of steady below zero [–18°C] temperature."

*Feb 3* "Went to the meadow and saw the Toole horses and they are looking pretty fair considering the condition they were in last fall."

Freer checked on the horses and did odds and ends throughout February. Jack George and John Porter came to purchase some groceries on February 16 and left the next day. Amos Alec and Frank George also came over.

*Feb 18* "I brought the rest of the Toole horses to the south pasture and am feeding them every day." Two days later Bridcut brought in Maggie Alec, Amos's daughter.

*Feb 21* "Marked out the plane landing at the overflow on the ice."

*Feb 22* "There is water on the plane landing now, overflow from Dust Creek. I made up a large grub order for Amos Alec for Turnagain River."

*Feb 23* "Bob Harrison of Watson Lake Flying Service came in with 1500 pounds of oats and Margaret and Maggie Alec and family and supplies to West Moodie Lake."

*Feb 24* "Amos Alec left for West Moodie Lake with his dogs."

Freer heard on March 5 that he would be working for Earl Boose on hunting trips from the middle of August to the end of September.

As the temperature became warmer in March, the west-facing hills became bare.

*Mar 17* "I fed the Toole horses in the south pasture on the hills here. Ann, Kim and Don are on the hills south of here."

Freer had a few similar entries in the following days.

In late March and early April, several people came to barter with Freer. Jack George and John Porter came from their trapping on March 23, bought supplies the next day, and returned to their trapline on March 25.

*Apr 1* "Amos Alec left for Turnagain River, took some grub."

*Apr 8* "Stan Bridcut came in from Watson Lake with my oats and returned to Watson with Amos Alec at Turnagain River. Jack and Frank George and John Porter came up from Horn Creek with one beaver and one wolf."

Freer observed some airplanes doing search and rescue work, including planes belonging to the United States Air Force.

*May 3* "A large jet plane went east and two search and rescue planes went south towards Vancouver. They had been looking for a downed plane near Snag in the Yukon."

*May 13* "A large 4 motor USAF plane crisscrossing the valley as though looking for a downed plane."

*May 17* Freer rode to Skook's place. "Skook is pretty well buggered up now." Two days later, he returned.

## SEARCH CONTINUES FOR MISSING PILOT

This was the headline for an article in the *Tallahassee* [Florida] *Democrat* newspaper on May 2, 1966. "Frank Hern, 39, left Fairbanks at 7:30 PM Thursday [April 28] and had expected to set a world record for a non-stop straight distance flight. He was flying a single-engine Cessna 150 and had only 150 gallons of gasoline aboard—a supply he hoped would last for the 3,500 mile [5,600 kilometre] flight to Tallahassee." The last radio contact with Hern was in the western Yukon after three hours of flight. The pilot reported that he was having difficulty with his radio transmitter.

On April 30, a search started for Hern and his plane. He had not filed a flight plan, which made searching more difficult and widened the area that needed to be covered. From May 1 to 15, an average of thirteen planes per day searched for Hern. There was national coverage of the event.

The wreckage of Hern's plane and the body of the pilot were finally spotted on September 26 in the western Yukon in a deep canyon from which the snow had recently melted.

In June, the men began to prepare for the hunting trips. Freer still did not have any work for the first part of the summer.

*June 18* "I went up town, no geological job for the horses and no hunting job neither, so shall head for home Monday."

Later in June, Willard had an accident while fording the Turnagain.

> *June 27* "Lost Jim and his full load. Seemed to sink and never saw him again. It was a deep ford. He had all the rope and canvas on."

Two days later, Skook came down with Art Swannell's helicopter and returned. Freer went to Skook's place, arriving at 11:00 p.m.

## *July 2–15 Watson Lake and Fireside*

On July 2, Freer went to Watson Lake and worked at Mac and Jac's for a week. Then he went to Fireside, but problems occurred with his boat.

> *July 9* "George Nelms and I took the boat and put it in the Liard River. We did not have time to try it out." When they did, on July 11, they found that the motor wouldn't operate properly. Freer took the motor to the mechanics at Fireside, but they couldn't repair it, so "George and I hauled all my stuff and cached it at George Nelms's place."

## *July 15–August 11 Prepare for hunters*

On July 17, Freer flew to the Kechika.

> *July 17* "Stan Bridcut picked me up at 4:30 AM. We went to the dock and the plane was gone. Jimmy Close was out and found a wrecked plane and two people drowned north of Watson Lake, so I didn't get out until 9 AM. Police had to go to the wrecked plane."

Freer spent the last week of July and the first week of August working around the camp.

> *Aug 7* "We tried to get the kicker running but no luck."

## *August 11–October 2 Hunting guide and packer for Skook Davidson*

> *Aug 11* Freer finally got started. "People in party: Bob and Harry Porter, Jack Davis, Yvonne Gauthier, Cook, and myself." They arrived at Forsberg Ridge the next day where they set up seven tents.

> *Aug 19* "We packed up and left Forsberg Ridge with 12 horse loads and camped in sheep area by a high pass."

During the following days, Freer and the hunters saw many sheep and goats and they shot a few. On August 23, they moved to Forsberg Lake, and from there they travelled to a campsite near caribou.

*Aug 28* "We hunted all day but saw nothing. We are sure covering a lot of country for nothing."

The weather was cold and rainy most days and the hunters didn't shoot any more game during the rest of their time.

*Sept 2* "Bob Harrison came in with the Beaver plane and took the hunters out. Bob had dinner with us. The horses were all in for the salt. The hunters were glad to get out."

Freer left for the caribou camp on September 4, arriving the next day in cold, wet weather after twelve hours of travel. The hunters stayed there until September 11. On September 19, they moved to Bennett camp. The hunters spent several days there and got sheep, goats and caribou. They started back to Forsberg Lake on September 25, arriving the next day. Three days later, they left for City Cabins.

*Sept 30* "Dempsey Alec and I left City cabins and arrived at Skook's in good time."

## October 2–12 Freer's cabin

*Oct 2* Bridcut flew Freer to his cabin. "My cache was broken into by taking the hinges off, pulled the nails." Freer spent a few days finding his horses and working around his cabin.

*Oct 10* "I cleaned up the place and came down river with Len Eklund and partner. They have been up the Frog River on a hunting trip and did all right, each had a sheep and 2 goats."

The next day, the men reached the mouth of the Kechika, and on October 12, Freer started working at Fireside. Margo was in Vancouver, and Ken was at Watson Lake for a few days, so they were probably glad to have Freer working at the lodge.

## October 12–December 31 Fireside

*Nov 6* "Margo and Ken arrived home from Dawson Creek."

In November and December, there were several accidents or vehicles that ran off the road because of the snow, and Fireside was busy. Fortunately, none of them were serious.

*Dec 17* The community "had a children's Christmas dinner at DPW Hall. I was Santa. Had a very good supper."

> *Dec 25* "The Nelms family were over and joined the Fireside Inn staff for Christmas dinner. It was a very good dinner. Very little traffic on the road. Cloudy and warm. Steve and Peggy Kirek came down to Christmas dinner with Dennis and Iris Kerik of DPW."

The end of the year was eventful at Fireside.

> *Dec 30* "Ken and Margo started for Smith River airport and were recalled because of the fire in the Annex. It caught fire somehow. Smouldered for five hours then burst into flames, caught fire at 5 PM. All the DPW boys came over to help us out. Everybody went home at 12 midnight as everything was burnt out, no damage to the other buildings."

> *Dec 31* "The Annex is still smouldering away. Not too busy here today. Margo and Ken went to Watson Lake for the New Year's Eve dance. The police came down from Watson Lake. Had a New Year's party here at DPW social club."

# 1967

## January 1–5 Fireside

Margo and Ken returned on January 2.

> *Jan 4* "I am finished as I am going home now to the Kechika River."

## January 6–May 25 Kechika River valley

On January 6, Freer flew back to his cabin. Freer found the horses to be in good condition, so he packed down the trails and sawed wood. From January 21 to 27, the temperature went below –40°C every night except one.

Freer had a few visitors in February, and Bridcut flew in with mail and groceries once. On March 5, Freer observed that the west-facing hills south of the ranch were starting to have some bare ground, so he put the government horses there. He also checked daily on two mares, June and May.

> *Mar 12* "I fed June and May their oats and sugar. They are starting to come back." Near the end of the month a WLFS plane brought in more supplies, including oats.

Once again, late March and April was the most difficult time of the year for the survival of the horses. While waiting for the grass to begin growing on the sunny hillsides, some horses needed to be fed.

*Apr 13* "I fed the usual horses oats, and they are having a tough time as the snow is so hard now."

Freer's birthday was on April 19, but he does not mention it in his diary, probably because of the event that occurred.

*Apr 19* "Went to feed June and May their oats and sugar and wolves killed June just before I arrived. Five wolves, blood all over the place. May is sure worried. The wolves must have come from up the valley, first sign I have seen. Ann and Kim are in the yard."

*Apr 20* "I was most of the day with May where the wolves killed a horse. Got all my clothes hanging around her." Freer observed that the wolves were still hanging around.

*Apr 22* "Saw the horses in the meadow and fed them. Ann and Kim in the yard. Went up and fed May. I dug a trail through the hard and deep snow to a bare side hill. The damn wolves are still hanging around the dead horses but won't touch them as I have too many clothes hanging around."

*Apr 23* "Went up and fed May her oats. She is sure lonesome. Fed Ann here and Kim in with her. I broke the trail out up to May through the snow. Will try to get her out tomorrow." Freer was successful in bringing May out, and he put her with some other horses.

Jack and Frank George visited in early May.

*May 6* "Jack George came down from up river to start trapping beaver." The next day he set out traps.

*May 8* "Frank George came down from up river at 4 AM, built a raft and Frank and Jack left by separate rafts for down river at 6 PM hunting beaver. They expect to float all the way to Fireside Mile 543 Alaska Highway."

Freer made his own raft on May 16 and enlarged it five days later.

*May 22* "I cleaned up everything and started down river for Fireside. It is pretty slow floating and the damn raft is no good." The next day he spent most of his time with the Government Water Resources Project crew that were putting a cable half a mile [800 metres] above Turnagain River on the Kechika River.

*May 25* "Arrived at Fireside about 9 PM on May 25. I had to line up the Liard which was tough lining. The Liard is rising fast."

### May 25–June 1 Fireside

Freer and Dennis, Margo's son, spent most of May 27 repairing Freer's boat motor.

### June 1–17 Government Water Resources Project

On June 1, Freer arrived at the water resources project camp. The next day, the crew began to build the water gauge station. This station would measure water flow on the Kechika above its largest tributary, the Turnagain. In the 1960s, there was discussion by the BC government about constructing a series of dams along the Liard River, similar to what was being done on the Peace River. Water gauge stations would be established at key locations throughout the Liard basin.

Freer worked on the water resources project for two weeks. His diary entries for the first half of June describe the details of the construction.

*June 13* "We worked on the main 1 1/8 inch cable all day. Put it across on one half inch cable with the winch. Some of the men did odds and ends. I was in the air at 41 feet most of the time on the tower."

*June 16* "Coast Range Airways was in with a Water Resources man and measured the water here on the cable car." The Water Resources project finished on June 17.

### June 17–July 23 Kechika River valley

Freer spent a week at his cabin. Then he made a raft to go down the Kechika on June 28, but a strong wind blew up the river, so he returned to his cabin.

*July 6* "I am trying to get the Mercury motor to run, but just sputters away. I don't know what is wrong."

*July 13* "I did nothing, still waiting for the plane to bring in my motor from Watson Lake."

*July 19* "Stan of Watson Lake Flying Service took Skook home and dropped me off at the cable station at the Turnagain River. He brought in my big kicker. I bailed water out of the boat and got everything off of the cache in readiness to load and go home tomorrow."

*July 20* "I loaded my boat and sure is a load too."

*July 21* "Put all my grub away that I brought up river."

The next day three hours and fifteen minutes of boat travel brought Freer to Skook's place. Some logjams in the Kechika made travel slow.

## July 24–31 Preparing for hunters

Skook had a large crew to handle the hunting trips he had booked, and on July 24, Freer joined them. The last week of July was spent making final preparations.

## August 1–September 26 Hunting guide and packer for Skook Davidson

*Aug 7* "Stan Bridcut was in after dinner with grub for my hunting party at Watson Lake. He brought in Margaret Boya as my cook and Frank George came back in to guide for me. I worked on my outfit most of the day."

On August 10, Freer left the Diamond J Ranch and reached the Broken Bit camp after seven hours of travel. For his group, Freer had Wayne Ball, Harry Porter, John Porter and Frank George, along with Margaret Boya as cook. Five days later, Watson Lake Flying Service took the hunters to Forsberg Lake. They hunted from that camp until leaving for Watson Lake on August 29.

On September 1, a group of four hunters arrived. The hunters in Freer's party got caribou, sheep and goats.

*Sept 5* "Saw a sheep 3 miles away, went after it and got it. It was 40 inches with a large base."

John Porter broke his ankle, so Freer sent two men from his crew with Porter out to Watson Lake the next day. On September 13, the hunters moved down to the Kechika River hunting camp to hunt bear. Two days later, a plane came in the evening to take the hunters out to Watson Lake.

On September 17, Freer arrived at Skook's ranch. Three days later Frank Cooke was over from Moodie Lakes with a hunter, John Caputo. Caputo was reputed to be a crime boss from New York. For many years he came to BC for big game hunting trophies. He brought his son, John Jr., a few times. Caputo hunted with several guide outfitters, and they have many stories about him.

Caputo is also mentioned in the BC Sessional Papers when he had an accident. The 1950 Provincial Game Commission report stated: "John Caputo, a non-resident hunter from New York, suffered a fractured leg when he fell between two fallen trees while running to get a shot at a grizzly. He recovered in the Fort St. John hospital after being flown out of the hunting territory."

Freer returned to his cabin on September 26.

### September 26–November 15 Kechika River valley

On October 9, Freer went to Skook's place.

> *Oct 15* "Len Eklund and partner, Bob, came down from up river where they had been hunting.... took my boat and went with them to my place for the night."

> *Oct 16* "Len got motor running good."

> *Oct 23* "A RCAF search and rescue plane with twin engines made the trip up the valley and back towards Watson Lake as though looking for a down plane. They were flying very low." (The airplane crashed on a flight from Fairbanks to Inuvik. It was missing for eight days before it was located. All three persons aboard survived.)

Freer went to Skook's cabin on October 26 and put six sheets of plywood on his floor. On the last day of the month, he returned to his cabin and spent a couple of weeks there. On November 13, Freer started for Skook's place where he planned to fly to Watson Lake and then go to work at Fireside.

> *Nov 13* "I am taking my cat with me as I cannot leave her."

On November 15, Freer reached Watson Lake and got a ride to Fireside.

### November 15–December 31 Fireside

The work was routine at Fireside throughout the rest of November and December. Freer noted that they were getting mail every day.

> *Dec 5* Freer went to a "picture show at the canteen." In mid-December Willard "went to Nelms and got my hair cut."

Christmas activities included a dinner and dance at the Department of Public Works (DPW) hall on December 16. The Roxboroughs had a party at their place on Christmas Eve.

> *Dec 25* "Everybody was over. Ken went up the road 15 miles to get a fellow out of the snow bank. The Nelms were over for Christmas dinner and Windrems went over to the Nelms's to play."

> *Dec 26* "Everybody from the DPW camp was over for a buffet style lunch supper and all the Fireside Inn staff was in."

# 1968

*January 1–August 18 Alaska Highway*

The year started with all the DPW camp personnel coming to the lodge for a New Year's dinner. The Alaska Highway did not have as much traffic in the winter, but at times it kept the personnel at Fireside busy, especially since it had a towing operation and a garage with a mechanic where flat tires could be fixed and vehicles repaired.

> *Jan 6* "Ken had to go to 558 for truck blocking the road yesterday. Vern went to 530 to pick up a small truck broke down. Christy's tanker returned from Lower Post and went on to Dawson Creek. Ken had to go to 555 to get a pickup truck out of the snow bank. The highway was very busy all day with car traffic."

Christy's fuel tanker continually drove from Dawson Creek to Lower Post, providing gasoline to locations along the highway.

> *Feb 6* "Max Scott, Christy's driver, came in with a load of fuel for DPW and some for here. DPW were out in force to get the road plowed and in shape…. The light plant blew up here."

In his diary, Freer mentions seeing a picture show on February 12 and 13. Movies were sent by bus to communities along the highway that had a recreation hall. George Nelms handled the movies at Fireside, and this was an important part of recreation in the community, particularly in the winter. The curling bonspiels continued to occur.

> *Feb 25* "Jim Plummerfelt and Sandy Taylor returned from the curling bonspiel at Muncho Lake. They both won prizes."

There were a couple of noteworthy events in March.

> *Mar 1* "A DPW man cut part of a finger off and they took him to Watson Lake by ambulance."

> *Mar 9* "There was a going away party for the DPW people as they are all leaving here around the end of this month. There was a curling round robin run off tonight at the curling club. Had a very good time and game and everything, plenty of the men were drunk, some quarrels."

The last week of the month was busy, as Nanaimo Bulldozing, which won the contract to maintain the section of the Alaska Highway in the Fireside area, began to bring in personnel.

*Mar 27* "Allied Van lines tractor is broke down. Did some welding and it left in the afternoon.... Ken and Margo arrived home in the evening glad to be back with the car. The first load of the new contractors, Nanaimo Bulldozing, arrived in camp today.... Vern pulled in a car from 502 mile post."

*Mar 28* "A Hill and Hill truck rolled at mile 535. Roy Shanberger was driving and had to go to Whitehorse by ambulance. Bill Cornish sent 2 tractors from Fort Nelson to pick up Fort Nelson lumber truck load."

*Mar 30* "I was real busy with the gas and odds and ends. Café fairly busy, some tires to fix, got all the Hill and Hill load reloaded and 2 tractors came in from Edmonton to pick up wrecked tractor and highboy with load. Ken and Margo went to Watson Lake to a farewell party for the postmasters there. Some of the Nanaimo Bulldozing crew came in to take over."

*Apr 1* "Quite busy all day with everything, lots of traffic, some flat tires to repair. The Nanaimo Bulldozing are increasing in strength all the time."

At the DPW compound, housing for families had been built, and Nanaimo Bulldozing brought in some personnel who had families.

*Apr 16* "There are plenty of children across the road as all the families are here now."

*Apr 17* About 7.5 centimetres of snow resulted in "seven car accidents, two head on collisions and some people sent to the hospital. The police were down. Our wrecker pulled in three cars from collision. Cloudy and cool and squally. Lots of accidents on the road between here and Watson. Lots of trucks on the road and a large twin rotor helicopter landed here because of stormy weather."

Freer's birthday was two days later, and this was one of the few times he had a celebration.

*Apr 19* "This is my birthday. We were quite busy here all day. Penny Swanson made a birthday cake for me and I went across to the Nelms and had another birthday cake and we played cards. The Keriks came over and George Miller came up from mile 408, his place."

A few days later, Freer noted the arrival of new technology in the community.

> *Apr 24* "CNT are here putting Telex machine. The Nanaimo Bulldozing came back with 3 new dump trucks and the family furniture."

Freer wrote about a robbery at Fireside.

> *May 6* "McDonald (Esso) station was broken into and the cash register was taken and a gun found. The man was caught at Fort Nelson. This man shot at a person... and hit him 4 times. The police were around here all day. The wounded fellow is in serious condition." Two days later, Freer wrote that the police were still at Fireside.

At the end of May, Freer noted the arrival of Joyce Nelms. She was studying in a master's program in sociology at the University of Victoria and her thesis was a study of the lives of the Indigenous people who lived at Lower Post. Joyce spent two summers at Lower Post. Freer loaned Joyce his dog, who provided a conversation starter.

## FIRESIDE: REMEMBERING THE PEOPLE

A number of people arrived at Fireside around 1960 who stayed for several years, bringing some stability to the community, which had previously been mainly populated by transient employees.

Jack and Flo Christy owned and operated lodges both at Lower Post and Fireside along the Alaska Highway for many years. In the late 1950s, they sold Fireside to Margo Windrem. Margo was born in Germany in 1913 and immigrated to Canada in the 1920s. Her first husband, Gerald McGannon, was a prospector, and they lived in Northwest Territories for a while before moving to Nanaimo. With financial help from her father, Margo purchased the East Wellington general store in the late 1940s. She added a post office and became the community's postmistress. Margo operated the store until the mid-1950s. During that time her marriage dissolved. Then she and a friend operated the commissary during the construction of the Crofton Pulp Mill on Vancouver Island. At that time, she met Ken Windrem. Ken, who was separated from his wife, had previously worked as a long-haul truck driver for Canadian National Telegraph for several years, so he was also familiar with life in northern Canada. Ken and his wife made a divorce settlement, and he then married Margo.

Ken and Margo Windrem. Windrem Family collection

George and Violet Nelms. Nelms Family collection

Margo purchased the Fireside Inn around 1959. While she managed the lodge and was postmistress, Ken handled the wrecking service and the mechanical operations at Fireside. He also booked in guests. Margo saw the potential to expand tourism along the Alaska Highway. She added a motel, made many upgrades, built accommodations for the employees, and got a community post office. There was a café, a dining room with a view of the Liard River, and a large pub. Margo was able to obtain overnight bookings for many bus tours, and she was considered the driving force in the development of Fireside. Margo's father, her son, Dennis, and Ken's son, Dale, worked at the lodge at various times. Margo and Ken operated the Fireside Inn business for about twenty years and had a good relationship with the residents of the community.

Dale Windrem and Joyce Nelms, serving as election officers for Fireside for a provincial election. The big stone fireplace is visible. Windrem Family collection

Around 1960, George Nelms, his wife, Violet, and their two youngest children came to Fireside. Born in England in 1907, George and his family immigrated to Canada in 1911. He grew up on a farm on the Prairies. In 1928, he married Clara Violet Rigler, and they had four children. George continued farming until 1944, when he and his family moved to northern BC, and he began to work for the Highways Department. George became maintenance foreman at locations along the Alaska

Highway. He and his wife would remain at Fireside during the 1960s until his retirement in the early 1970s.

The Nelms played an active role in the Fireside community. Once a week there was a movie at the recreation centre, and George was the projectionist. Violet was the assistant postmistress and ran the post office when Margo was away.

Willard began working at Fireside in the fall of 1960 after he finished his third summer of packing for the Geological Survey of Canada. Since he had worked for Flo and Jack Christy over several years, they would have recommended him to Margo and Ken. Like most lodges along the Alaska Highway, there was almost continuously a shortage of employees, so Willard always received employment whenever he wanted to work there. At Fireside, Willard took care of the gas pumps, shovelled snow in the winter, and did a variety of handyman jobs. When he worked at Fireside in the winter, the Windrems would sometimes leave for a few weeks' vacation.

Willard Freer at the gas pumps. Nelms Family collection

Percy Nelms. Nelms Family collection

June was a quiet month until the last week. Margo received a phone call that her father had had a heart attack, and she went to be with him at Stony Plain near Edmonton. There was a federal election on June 25, so "no liquor of any kind." (This was Pierre Trudeau's first term as prime minister of Canada.) At the end of the month, the hamburger stand at Liard Hot Springs started operating for the summer.

> *Aug 1* "Went to Burnt Rose Lake to see Earl Boose and will be hunting for Earl at Starvation Lakes starting August 20 to October 20. The plane brought me back to my place." Earl's guiding area was north of Skook's, and some of it was part of Freer's trapline.

> *Aug 10* "Len Eklund and partner, Bob, arrived by boat from Fort St. John on a hunting trip on the upper Kechika, Frog and Gataga rivers. They stayed here overnight."

*August 18–September 26 Packer and hunting guide for Earl Boose*
Freer left his cabin at Horneline Creek on August 18.

> *Aug 21* "I finally made my Lake Camp at 1 PM. Horses down in the mud. Took the hunters to the Moose Lake, saw some nice moose but nothing that the hunter wanted."

> *Aug 24* "The Beaver plane brought in 2 hunters and Indian guides from Burnt Rose Lake. The plane had quite a job of getting in because of the stormy weather and very low ceiling, had to roundabout. Plane returned to Watson Lake. Very heavy rain." It rained every day, limiting the hunting the men did.

> *Aug 30* "The plane came in just at dusk and brought in 2 hunters and left with 2 hunters." The men hunted for the next week.

> *Sept 6* "The plane arrived at 9 AM and took the hunters and guides to Burnt Rose Lake to start sheep and goat hunting there. They report they expect to camp there for 2 weeks."

> *Sept 14* "Watson Lake Flying Service plane arrived at 8 AM with 2 hunters and guides. I took a fly camp up to the caribou camp."

The hunters stayed at this camp for five days. Then they moved to Willard Lake where an airplane arrived on September 21 to take out the hunters and guides. On September 26, Freer departed, and he arrived at his cabin three days later.

### September 26–November 30 Kechika River valley and Alaska Highway

Oct 16 "John McCook and son and Frank George came down from Gataga Forks where they are going to trap. They bought a bunch of grub and camped here for the night."

Oct 20 Freer went to visit Skook and stayed for two nights. "Skook and I just laid around and talked and read quite a lot. Some sheep and goat on the hill here. The work team was in for oats."

Nov 3 "I went up to No. 6 looking around and plenty of wolf sign and they are staying right with the horses."

Nov 13 "John McCook and wife and boy were down for some groceries. They returned to Gataga Forks where they are trapping and the rest of the family is."

Nov 17 Freer saw one of the old government horses from the original 1939 herd. "Saw the 2 government horses in the meadow, the old Grey one is pretty thin, I doubt if he will see the new year."

Nov 24 "Stan Bridcut of Watson Lake Flying Services went to Skook's with the super cub and landed at my place on ice. Took off and landed on sand bar. I went to Watson with him, stayed at Jack and Mac's motel, $7." Freer worked at Fireside for almost a week.

Nov 29 "Went over to Nelms and my haircut and played crib. I was the winner."

### December 1–31 Peace River district

A Christy's fuel tanker arrived from Dawson Creek, bringing gas and diesel. Freer went back to Dawson Creek with him because he wanted to have his dog spayed. Willard stayed with his brother Frank at his farm.

Dec 4 Freer took his dog to the vet. "Saw quite a few people I used to know. Haven't seen some of them since 1931."

Dec 5 "There was a cancellation at the optometrist and I got my eyes tested for new reading classes. Cost $45. We stayed around Fort St. John. Had a few drinks, met some of the old-timers. I saw Mabel Frank."

*Dec 6* "Frank, Georgia and I went to Fort St. John. We shopped around and had supper at the Condill hotel. I got my dog back, $22.50. She looks good."

*Dec 7* "Frank, Georgia and I went to Hudson Hope. Saw nobody I know. We had supper at Georgia's brother's place toward the Portage Mountain Dam. Saw it. There are 3 generators running. The lake above the dam is all open water in the lake."

During the following days, the Freers met and visited several people, including Nels Westergaard, Duncan Beatton and Don Peck.

*Dec 19* "We went to town, picked up Edith [Frank's daughter] and had supper and went to the Halfway River to the school concert. It was very good. Santa Claus came for the children, then supper and dancing."

*Dec 25* "Nobody did much of anything. Dave and Carol Ronine and family came from Beryl Prairie west of Hudson Hope for Christmas dinner. There was lots of Christmas presents. They returned home at 10 PM."

# 1969

### January 1–11 Peace River district

Freer stayed with his brother in early January. During that time "my dog ran into a porcupine and got 6 quills in her nose," he wrote. Freer had trouble getting a ride back to Fireside, and it was not until January 12 that he finally arrived there.

### January 12–February 1 Watson Lake

Freer spent a couple of days recovering from the flu before going to Watson Lake on January 15.

*Jan 27* "The Watson Lake trading Post caught fire and burned to the ground. Nothing was saved at all.... Apparently the wood furnace caught fire in the basement and nobody could do anything.... Had 2 fire engines there, so cold the heat went up and never scorched building 50 feet [15 metres] away. I was over after and it is sure a mess."

*Jan 31* "The Jac and Mac's motel has been sold to new people from Prince George and take over tomorrow. There was a going away party sponsored by the old owners Mac and Jac Stanker in the cocktail lounge. The drinks were all on the house and the bar was sure full. It was a great going away party."

Inclement weather prevented airplane flights from Watson Lake until February 1.

### February 1–June 6 Kechika River valley

Freer quickly settled into the usual work around his cabin.

*Feb 7* "Frank George came down from Gataga River where he is trapping with John McCook. They aren't doing much trapping, too damn cold."

*Feb 8* "Frank George fixed up his sleigh and went up river at noon and returned to John McCook's trapping camp."

*Feb 17* "Stan Bridcut of Watson Lake Flying Service went to Skook's and landed here with the Beaver and took out my mail. Corrie Reimer, pilot of the Watson Lake Flying Service had the Cessna 180 come up from the Turnagain where he has the Water Resources. He had coffee."

*Mar 6* "Jack George and brother Stan was down from Cottonwood Flats and got some grub and returned."

*Mar 9* "John McCook and 2 of his children were down from Gataga River and got some grub and paid most of his bill of over $300 by cash and some fur."

Near the end of the month, WLFS pilot Corrie Reimer stopped for coffee.

By the beginning of April, the snow was melting. Some of the hills became bare, and a few of the horses went there to feed.

*Apr 5* "The wolves were sure howling close by here last night and today."

*Apr 18* Freer's next visitor arrived. "Dempsey Alec was over from Amos Alec on the Turnagain River. He had a saddle horse and returned to the Turnagain."

*May 4* Freer "was around the cabin in the afternoon and

stretching beaver. John McCook and son and a Massetoe boy had 13 beaver. Frank George came with Ernest Abou and Brian Porter with 5 beaver, all green."

*May 5* "I bought fur from all these Indians. They got groceries and returned up the valley." Freer describes several transactions with the Indigenous trappers during beaver trapping in May.

*May 24* "I chored around here all day, did some baking and baled up my fur. Charlie Pete baled his fur for shipment. The Indians sprung their beaver traps as the river is rising too fast."

The Indigenous people remained at Freer's for a week, waiting for an airplane.

*June 1* "The Indians are getting anxious to get out."

*June 3* "Charlie Boya and Charlie Pete went to Skook's with a saddle horse and returned. They went up to see what is wrong about a plane to get this bunch of Indians out." The plane finally arrived on the evening of June 5.

### June 6–December 31 Alaska Highway and trips on Kechika River

Freer was unable to obtain fieldwork during the summer of 1969, so he worked at Fireside and took some trips up the Kechika River.

*June 6* "Stan Bridcut of Watson Lake flying service was in with the super cub at 8 AM and picked me up, came to Watson Lake, shipped my Beaver and caught a ride with Loiselle Transport to Fireside. They're quite busy here at Fireside. Saw the Nelms, they have a boat for me."

*June 7* "George Nelms and I tried to get the gale kicker to work, but runs rough."

Freer wrote about all the activity at Fireside during June.

*June 11* "The gas and café were sure busy today. There were plenty of flat tires too."

*June 15* "We were real busy with everything, sure lots of gas and traffic on the road. Plenty of flat tires and other mechanical stuff to do. Rooms and café was very good."

*June 19* "Helped a Loiselle driver unload 20 ton of cement and some lumber here for the Water Resources."

*July 7* "3 Water Resources boys lost their boat and kicker and one man nearly drowned at the whirlpool. A fellow swam out and saved one man."

On July 19, Freer began a trip up the Kechika with Dennis Kerik.

*July 19* "George Nelms, Dennis Kerik and I put the boat in at mile 547 and tried out the kicker and went to Honeymoon Island and back. Dennis and I started up the Kechika River and camped at Red River." The two men arrived at Freer's place the next day. After spending a day there, the men returned on July 22.

*July 22* "We stopped at the goose camp for dinner and broke the 25 horse Gale at the Lone Sister, and put the 33 Johnson motor on."

*Aug 1* "Len Eklund and wife came up from Fort St. John with their boat and 2 other boys came up with their boat with a 65 hp and 35 hp."

*Aug 18* "Another small crew came into work on the proposed dam site [on the Liard River] at mile 552."

*Aug 19* "Len Eklund and wife returned from their hunt up the Kechika River with one small goat. I bought the boat."

*Aug 20* "The small tanker was in from Fort Nelson with 1000 gallons No. 2 gas and 500 diesel and a 25 gallon barrel oil. Dale and Mrs. Hall went to Watson and returned with Waterhouse car. The beer truck came in with 200 cases beer.... Margo's son arrived with family from Nanaimo BC."

Freer noted the provincial election on August 27 in which W.A.C. Bennett was re-elected as premier. That fall, Fireside had Mrs. Brown as teacher for the school.

*Oct 7* "We were fairly busy here, Margo putting very long hours and so am I. Am on the pumps and the bar."

*Oct 10* "We were real busy here all day. I sure fuelled up a lot of trucks. The fuel tanker unloaded and returned to Fort Nelson. Café and rooms were very busy. Lots of trucks stayed for the night."

It snowed on October 20 and 21 and the roads were slippery. A week later, Freer wrote that NBC (Nanaimo Bulldozing Company) was making a skating rink and a curling rink.

> *Oct 31* "Lots of people on the road and all are stopping for the night as rain and very slippery. NBC crew never got in until 9 PM as the hills north were too wet. Trucks were leaving trailers on the road so couldn't keep vehicles on the road even with all wheels chained."

> *Nov 1* "The NBC crew were out sanding the road. Very wet and slippery. Lots of people in the ditch."

> *Nov 11* "I went to Nelms, got my haircut and over to the Kerik's for coffee at night."

> *Nov 16* "Margo sure is putting in very long hours as there is no help. I helped with the dishes along with the gas and odds and ends." There was a picture show at the canteen on November 24. In early December, Freer contracted chicken pox, and he was sick for several days.

> *Dec 25* "The Nelms and George Miller were over for Christmas dinner. Ken and Margo went over to the Nelms after supper and everything was cleaned up."

> *Dec 26* "Went over to the Nelms for Christmas for turkey dinner. It was very nice."

# THE 1970s: 1970–1975

## HIGHLIGHTS

From 1970 to 1975, most of Freer's diary describes routine activities. Special or unusual events are included in the quotations in this section. At the beginning of this decade, Freer began having health problems. He contracted chicken pox, and in the aftermath, had problems with fluid in his ears. This limited his activities, and he stayed close to his cabin or at Fireside. It took several operations over a few years before his ear problem was successfully resolved.

From 1973 to 1975, the last years for which Freer's diaries exist, he experienced a rejuvenation of his career. The BC government launched a forest inventory project and needed many workers. Freer obtained employment as a cook and boatman. For the last two field seasons, Freer worked about five months each year. He spent all three summers at locations in BC where he had not worked or visited previously.

During the 1970s, Freer still bartered furs with the Indigenous inhabitants of the Kechika, spending at least a couple of months at his cabin, which he always considered his home.

## 1970

*January 1–March 25 Fireside*

The new year started with Nanaimo Bulldozing holding a party at the recreation hall. In mid-January, the temperature went below −40° for a few days.

> *Jan 12* "There is a truck froze up at mile 558 and a car stuck there. Ken and Joe are trying to get the well to operate as we are out of water. Ken got the water running again. Had to get water from across the road."

> *Jan 13* "Lots of people stuck here today as the vehicles would not start, too damn cold. Pulled in two cars here from Coal River and one truck from 558. Everything is freezing up. Water lines froze up here and also the sewer."

> *Jan 14* "Some of the trucks were taken over to NBC to be thawed out. Sure lots of traffic on the road. Also vehicles are freezing up as too damn cold. Lots of people laid over as too cold and froze up. We ran out of beer here.... Ben Abel was working on our light plant that broke down."

*Jan 15* "Several trucks tied up here, too cold." This diary entry also mentioned "J.J. Cramer, the horse rider from New York." Cramer stayed around Fireside during the cold weather and resumed his journey on January 23.

## J.J. CRAMER

In 1969 and 1970, J.J. Cramer made a trip by horseback from Middleport, in western New York, to Juneau, Alaska. Cramer and his horse, Doc, began their journey of more than 8,000 kilometres on May 23, 1969. They received considerable publicity in American and Canadian newspapers as people followed their progress.

On August 6, Cramer arrived in Sioux City, Iowa, where the local paper ran an article. The reporter wrote: "Cramer is 'roughing it' the best he can. He never sleeps in a house at night, usually ends up in a barn, a truck, trailer or some horse outbuilding. Sometimes he sleeps under the stars…. When it comes to rein in for the night, he looks for a place that has horses, where he can inevitably establish a rapport with fellow horse owners. He says he's never been turned down for a place to stay and bed his horse."

Cramer arrived in Billings, Montana, on September 19. From there he headed northwest to Browning, a small community near Glacier National Park that was not too far from the border with Canada. Cramer entered Canada at the Piegan-Carway border crossing, and by October 22, he had reached Calgary, where he stayed on the Stampede grounds. Continuing north, he reached Edmonton on November 3. His route then went northwest to Dawson Creek, Mile 0 on the Alaska Highway.

About 300 kilometres north along the Alaska Highway, Cramer had a misfortune, which was described in the *St. Joseph* (Missouri) *News Press*. "A man who left Middleport, NY in the spring to travel to Alaska has lost his means of conveyance—his horse—after riding nearly 4,000 miles [6,400 kilometres]. J.J. Cramer tied his horse outside and went to sleep in a shack 120 miles [200 kilometres] south of this northcentral British Columbia community [Fort Nelson]. When he awoke, the animal was gone. Cramer believes the horse may have been scared off by wolves."

With the assistance of local people, Cramer found Doc, and he resumed his trip along the Alaska Highway. When Cramer arrived at Fireside in mid-January, the temperature was around −40°C, so he stayed for about ten days. Cramer was in Whitehorse in February and arrived in Juneau in March, completing an epic journey that took nine months and six days.

J.J. Cramer on horse that he rode from New York to Alaska. Lockport New York Museum

*March 25–September 5 Kechika River valley*

On July 5, Freer wrote that he had not been feeling well for the past week. This was the beginning of health problems for Freer. He had had chicken pox the previous December, and sometimes there are complications for the health of older people as a result. On July 7, Freer wrote in his diary that he felt sick, and there are several notations in the following days regarding his ill health.

> *July 16* "I did nothing all day as I was too sick, too hard to move. Tried to flag down Beaver plane that went to Skook's in morning but no luck." Unfortunately for Freer, his radio was not working, so he was unable to call for assistance.

> *July 18* "I did practically nothing as I felt so sick. Have been this way for a month. Will have to get out of here."

> *Aug 1* "I sure wish I could get better. I want to get out, but scared to move."

> *Aug 17* "Len Eklund and partner arrived from Fireside on their yearly hunt. They came up in around eight hours with two motors running. They stayed the night here." Eklund and partner departed the next day.

*September 5–12 Fireside*

Eklund and his partner returned from their hunting trip on September 4. Len had to come out early because he broke glass in his hand and needed to get it treated. The next day the three of them came down the river. Freer stopped at Fireside.

*September 12–29 Fort Nelson*

On September 12, Freer went to Fort Nelson. Two days later, he saw Dr. Kenyon, who took some head x-rays and prescribed some medication. Freer went back to Fireside on September 29 because he was going to Edmonton in October to see a specialist.

*September 29–October 13 Preparations and trip to Kechika River valley*

*October 14–31 Fireside*

The second half of October was a difficult time at Fireside. On October 19 Margo had to go to Edmonton for her father was quite sick. On October 27 the staff house burned down at midnight. Cabins C1 and C2 caught fire but the fire was put out. The same day, Margo's dad died.

*Oct 29* "Ken went to Watson Lake and flew to Edmonton for Margo's dad's funeral. 2 car collision at mile 562 and 2 stretcher victims. Had to have 2 ambulances to Watson Lake. Had to have both cars in too for storage as they are a total loss. All the people were taken to Watson Lake to the hospital."

Ken and Margo returned on October 31. The next day Freer left for Edmonton.

## November 1–13 Edmonton

Freer arrived in Edmonton on November 3 and had an appointment with a physician who told him he was supposed to go to the hospital tomorrow for there was fluid in his ear. Freer spent about five hours at the University Emergency Ward the next day while the physician treated his ear. The following day Freer wandered around Edmonton.

*Nov 5* "Sure is a mad rat race around with the cars."

On his follow-up visit the next day, the physician told Freer that he was satisfied with the operation and could leave.

## November 14–December 31 Fireside

*Dec 19* "There was a Christmas party for the kids, a turkey dinner for everyone. There were quite a few drunk."

*Dec 20* "Johnny Forsberg stole NBC grader at Contact Creek, slammed into a Lynden truck."

*Dec 25* "Had a very good Christmas dinner. The Nelms were over and some of the staff here. The Nelms showed slides from Joyce's trips around the Orient."

# 1971

## January 1–February 19 Fireside

*Jan 1* "There was a big New Year's Eve party across the road last night, and nobody is feeling too good today. Quite a few in the beer parlour."

On January 3, Mrs. Brown, the schoolteacher, returned. School started the next day and there was a community picture show in the evening.

*February 19–June 22 Kechika River valley*

> *Feb 19* "George Nelms took me to Watson Lake Flying Service and Stan Bridcut brought me home to the Kechika. A very nice day. Clear and clouding over. Saw some of my horses in the hills as I flew over."

Freer had returned earlier than usual, and he spent the first days cleaning up around the cabin and shovelling out the trails. In the late spring, Freer wrote about an incident with wolves.

> *May 31* "Amos [Alec] dug out a wolf pup, gave Louis two and kept one, killed 5 pups."

> *June 1* "The mother wolf of destroyed pups was in Indian camp after 2 pups there."

> *June 4* "Shot the wolf pups, saw the old mother."

As the month continued, Freer wrote that he didn't do much work because his ear was bothering him.

> *June 6* "Baled up all my beaver and am going to try to get them out."

> *June 11* Freer went to visit Skook at his ranch; Skook "is pretty well crippled up."

Freer had an unusual visit on June 13.

> *June 13* "A helicopter stopped here and they are taking the census from Cassiar. The RCMP are doing it."

> *June 15* "A Cessna with Stan WLFS went to Skook's and stopped here and on to Burnt Rose Lake. They are taking the census."

## June 22–July 25 Fireside

On June 22, Freer arrived at Fireside and worked there until he left for Fort Nelson on July 4. The physician told him that he needed to go to Edmonton again. Freer resumed working at Fireside until July 25, when he travelled to Edmonton by bus.

## July 25–August 4 Edmonton

> *July 28* "Saw Dr. Lupin and he confirms it. My ear is the same as last November, only worse. Will operate tomorrow."

After the operation, Freer remained in Edmonton until August 2.

*Aug 4* "Arrived Fireside at 1 AM and started on the gas pumps again."

## August 4–October 24 Fireside

August saw the arrival of the Fiennes expedition, which intended to travel across British Columbia from north to south through wilderness areas.

*Aug 9* "There is a bunch of English people here that were on the Nahanni valley. They are on the Liard and going up to Kechika River over to the Finlay and out by Prince George."

*Aug 10* "The Limeys are still here."

*Aug 13* "The English expedition started up the Kechika River."

Two days later, Freer wrote that he met Len Eklund, who came down the Kechika where he had been on his annual hunting trip. His partner left him, so he was by himself.

*Aug 16* "Len Eklund and I went with Len's boat down the Smith and the Liard rivers and picked up my boat that got loose from mile 540, put my boat at 540. Len took off for Fort St. John. George Nelms picked me up at Smith River.... My boat not damaged at all."

*Aug 17* "All of the English bunch are here. They never got too far." In the book *The Headless Valley* that Fiennes wrote, he describes getting lost in the upper Kechika and having to return to Fireside. Ironically, they had not talked to Freer, who knew the location of the Davie Trail.

A special event marked the completion of the branch line of the Pacific Great Eastern (PGE) railway from Prince George to Fort Nelson.

*Sept 9* "Ken and Margo left for Fort Nelson at 5 PM to take in the celebration put on by the PGE Railway arrival there tomorrow." Ken and Margo returned on September 12.

*Sept 15* Ken's son, Dale, "left for Victoria and on to California to go to school."

*Oct 4* "The police were down chasing a car and caught it at mile 523, took man prisoner and Ken hauled stolen car to here. Picked up Guy Merchant and McDonald of Imperial Esso for stealing light plant from Bryson at the Hyland River."

*Oct 5* "The Nelms returned from their holiday down at Williams Lake. They have been gone over a month. They were working on their piece of land there." George was retiring soon. The Nelms had purchased property in the Cariboo and planned to live there.

### October 24–November 4 Edmonton

Freer went to Fort Nelson on October 24 and from there flew to Edmonton.

*Oct 28* "I went to the University Hospital and had my ear fixed at 11:30 AM. Was in hospital about 4 hours waiting." On November 2, Freer flew back to Fort Nelson. Two days later, George Nelms took Freer back to Fireside.

*Nov 4* "I started on the pumps at once. Margo and Ken left for Vancouver."

### November 4–December 31 Fireside

*Dec 25* "Very quiet Christmas. Had a small party for Joyce Nelms across the road. This is a farewell party as she will not be up this way again."

*Dec 27* "George Nelms took Joyce to Watson and flew back to her job at Williams Lake. Everybody went to the picture show."

*Dec 28* "Most of the people went to the Walt Disney show for the kids." The following evening there were two curling games.

*Dec 31* "Everybody went to the New Year's Eve party at the recreation hall in the road camp."

# 1972

### January 1–April 22 Fireside

Continuing health problems related to his ear limited Freer's activities during 1972.

There were celebrations for the New Year at Fireside.

*Jan 1* "Had all the children from the road camp for lunch and small gifts. Most of the adults were over for drinks and midnight supper, open house at Fireside."

*Jan 2* "Most of the people had a good time and plenty of headaches [from] the open house here at Fireside."

Life at Fireside was uneventful until January 14.

*Jan 14* "All phones and telex out of order. 3 CNT men here repairing the phones."

Freer wrote about an important event four days later.

*Jan 18* "Skook Davidson had a house fire and lost all his personal stuff." This fire dramatically ended Skook's time at his beloved ranch.

*Jan 24* "The waterlines froze up. Mike and Fred got water running. Lots of cars on the road and plenty are freezing up. GCP [the highway maintenance crew] never worked, too cold. Everything here was real busy."

*Jan 25* "We were quite busy here all day as all the traffic having trouble of freezing up. The water was off again. GCP never worked, too cold."

*Jan 26* "Ken finally got another light plant running."

*Mar 2* "A jet helicopter landed here for lunch, it was from Anchorage going to California." During the first weekend in March, Fireside hosted a small bonspiel.

*Mar 4* "Had a farewell party for the Nelms…. The party broke up at 6 AM, everybody seemed to have a good time."

The diary entries from March 11 to April 23 are missing. Probably the main event was the retirement of George Nelms at the end of March. Freer likely remained at Fireside until George and Violet left. He had had a good friendship with the Nelms for more than ten years and probably would not see them very often in the future. The entry for April 24 indicates that Freer had just returned to the Kechika valley within the last day or two.

*April 22–August 17 Kechika River valley*

On April 30 and on May 2, Stan Bridcut brought in food for Freer. Freer returned for spring beaver trapping, but he missed some of the preparations and was not involved with as many people as he had been in previous years.

> *July 27* "Harry Porter walked down from Skook's for some stuff.... Skook is in Whitehorse Hospital, some say he won't be back and he is in a wheelchair."

> *July 30* "Len Eklund and partner, and another boat with 3 fellows came up from Fort St. John to hunt. They will make Gataga River and hunt out from there." Eklund was on his annual trip to the Kechika.

*August 17–September 12 Edmonton; return to Fireside*

On August 17, Freer travelled down the Kechika River with Eklund to Fireside. The next day, Freer wrote that he had a bad headache most of the day and was waiting for a doctor's appointment to go to Edmonton to have his ear examined. A week later, he received a letter stating that he had an appointment scheduled for August 29. Freer met the physician, who had an operation scheduled on the last day of the month. Freer remained in Edmonton during Labour Day weekend.

> *Sept 2* "Wandered around town most of the day looking around, looking and watching the mad rush of the cars. One collision I saw. Commercial hotel was robbed of $100 but caught the guy."

On September 6, Freer flew to Fort Nelson where he stayed with his friends, Paul and Donna Rivest, until September 12 when he travelled by bus to Fireside.

*September 12–25 Preparations and travel up Kechika to Freer's cabin*

*September 25–December 31 Kechika River valley*

On October 2, Frank George arrived from the Diamond J. He told Freer that Skook was still in Vancouver, and that he and Kenny Porter were looking after the ranch. In mid-October, Kenny Porter arrived.

> *Oct 14* "Skook has been in Vancouver since July and sort of lost his memory, not likely he will be back. His nephew from Calgary is supposed to be in charge of things."

Trapping started in early November. In early December, some of the Indigenous trappers stopped at Freer's cabin.

*Dec 22* "Amos Alec arrived here at 8 PM from Dall Lake on the Turnagain River. Amos and family came on West Moodie Lake drainage to Turnagain River."

*Dec 23* "Amos Alec laid over here today. He cleaned out his winter trail. I chored around, got grub ready for Amos." On Christmas Eve, Alec left for his family and trapline.

*Dec 25* "Christmas day and nobody around at all."

## 1973

This was a year of change and new activity in the Kechika River valley. It was a year since the fire at the Diamond J Ranch, and it was obvious that Skook would be unable to return from Vancouver. This marked the end of over thirty years living in the Kechika River valley for Skook, and his guiding territory was sold to Gary Moore. Both Moore and Frank Cooke Jr. at Scoop Lake, near Freer's place, spent time and money improving their facilities. Freer wrote several times about hearing construction at Cooke's base camp. A man and a woman leased land and built a cabin about a kilometre from Freer's place. They brought friendship and controversy to Freer and the Indigenous inhabitants of the valley. In 1973, there was finally an improvement in Freer's health, enabling him to obtain employment with the BC Forest Service for a few months. The work took him to a part of BC he had not previously visited.

*January 1–August 26 Kechika River valley*

*Jan 1* "January and the new year sure came in with a real bang. A real heavy northern blizzard blew hard all day with driving snow," wrote Freer at his cabin in the Kechika valley.

On January 14, Freer wrote that a DC-3 airplane from Arctic Air at Fort Nelson had landed at Scoop Lake. Frank Cooke Jr., who had the guiding territory on the west side of the Kechika River valley, was making improvements to his base camp at the lake, including a light plant. Arctic Air brought supplies several times over the winter. Freer could hear the airplane at Scoop Lake and the construction work. Later that year, Judy Drake and Ed Johnson arrived on a Watson Lake Flying Service plane.

*Apr 10* A WLFS plane "landed here with Judy Drake and Ed Johnson from Vancouver. They are intending to lease land around here and stay." Their arrival occurred while the Indigenous inhabitants were busy trapping. "We packed all their stuff off of the river.... Ed and Judy put up a tent."

During the next two days the three people looked at potential sites to build a cabin.

*Apr 13* "We moved most of Ed Johnson and Judy Drake's stuff and equipment up river one half mile where they are going to build a temporary cabin."

*Apr 19* For Freer's birthday "Judy Drake made a very good supper. They brought over a birthday present for me."

In the following days, Freer's diary recorded Ed and Judy's activities along with the trapping of the Indigenous people.

*May 4* "The Indians were around all day skidding and stretching their beaver that they got yesterday. They also got 4 black wolf pups yesterday across the river. They went out today and just got one small one. Judy and Ed were down for supper. They bought one wolf pup $75." Two days later Ed and Judy bought a second one, and eventually they had three wolf pups. In mid-May Freer had several visitors that he noted in his diary.

*June 7* "Skook has been out for a year now and the place has been sold. He will never be back."

Freer noted that a BC Forest Service boat was about 1.6 kilometres down the river on June 8 and 9. This boat was involved in a provincial forest inventory project. The BC government had several crews working on sites around BC over several years. In 1973, the Kechika was one of the valleys that was being inventoried. On June 14, Freer wrote that four students with three canoes who had gone to the headwaters of the Gataga River a week ago were camping at his place.

*June 15* "The 4 canoes in from yesterday had breakfast here, went up to see the old Dust cabin of Klondiker days and continued their trip down river. They will stop at Scoop Lake today."

*June 17* "I didn't do much today as my ear is bad, running liquid." Fortunately, Freer recovered.

*June 29* "The forestry boat and 3 men went up river from Scoop Lake where their base camp is. Sure lots of planes all over." On the last day of the month, Freer packed and labelled his fur to go out with Ed and Judy.

On July 26, Freer wrote that planes were ferrying supplies from Scoop Lake to the hunting camps in Mac Cooke's guiding area.

> *July 31* "Lots of planes around with floats on. Some of them are bringing in hunters for the Big Bang that will go off tomorrow, August 1, 1973."

> *Aug 1* "The big hunt has started today for sheep and goats. No game around."

> *Aug 9* "One forestry boat returned from Denetiah Creek to Scoop Lake. They want me to run a government boat on the Stikine River near Telegraph Creek. Supposed to let me know tomorrow." The next day he heard that his work wouldn't start for about two weeks. He also met Len Eklund on his annual hunt in the Kechika valley.

### August 26–October 22 Forest Inventory Project, Stikine River area

> *Aug 23* The "forestry helicopter landed to let me know that I must be ready to go to work Sunday, August 26. The forestry is to pick me up here."

On August 28, Freer arrived at Bell-Irving River. Three days later, he flew to a camp on the Stikine River. During the main part of summer, students did most of the work on the forest inventory crews. Around Labour Day these people returned to their education, and the Forest Service needed to hire replacements for the last part of the summer field season. One of the supervisors for the forest inventory survey in the Kechika River valley, probably Pete Small, must have noticed Freer's ability to handle large riverboats, cook, and work around camp, and recommended him for employment for the remainder of the field season.

During September, Freer moved the forestry workers by boat to their inventory stations. In the first week of the month, most of the work was along the Stikine River. In his diary, Freer provides details of his activities.

On October 4, Freer and the men left Wrangell at 7:00 a.m. on the forestry boat *Hecate Ranger*. They arrived in Prince Rupert at 3:00 p.m., picked up a vehicle and drove to Bell-Irving camp on the Stewart-Cassiar highway. Freer spent a week there packing equipment and cleaning the place. He arrived in Watson Lake on October 20 and flew back to the Kechika two days later.

*October 22–December 31 Kechika River valley*

During November, Freer spent most of his time working around his cabin. He was having difficulty in his relationship with Ed and Judy because the tame wolves were very destructive, chewing almost all of Freer's leather goods and any loose objects. Freer has many references describing the damage Judy and Ed's wolves caused. He noted that Ed and Judy were packing meat for the wolves from the moose that Frank George shot. Freer also commented on the industrial noise from Cooke's operations at Scoop Lake, noting that the light plant there was running twenty-four hours a day almost every day.

December was quiet at Freer's place except for the wolves and the havoc they created.

> *Dec 25* "I didn't do much at all. Ed and Judy were down for Christmas dinner. Judy made the dinner and it was very nice, had a bottle of liquor and played some cribbage, a quiet day. Those damn wolves raising hell all day. I'll have to do something."

> *Dec 27* "Jack, Don, Frank George came down from up river and had supper here. Ed and Judy and the god damn wolves were over. They sure chewed up stuff here. The Indians brought down two dog sleighs and stayed at their cabin down below. Ed, Judy and I finished off the Christmas turkey."

## 1974

*January 1–10 Kechika River valley*

On New Year's Day, Freer went to Ed and Judy's place for supper.

> *Jan 2* The wolves "haven't been over here for three days now, thank goodness, nice and peaceful." However, the next day he resumed his complaints about the wolves in his diary.

The tame wolves created a difficult situation for Ed and Judy. Many of the Indigenous people were upset that Ed and Judy were keeping captive wolves because they believed that the wolves should be part of the natural world and not kept in a domestic setting. Willard liked Ed and Judy's friendship, but he was upset at the damage that the wolves did to his equipment.

It's difficult to understand why Ed and Judy weren't more sensitive and respectful to the feelings of the inhabitants of the valley. Freer has many diary entries complaining about the wolves. After three decades of quiet life in the Kechika River valley, the tame wolves and the development and modernization of the facilities at Scoop Lake Outfitters changed the tranquility around Freer's place. Over forty years later, Darwin Cary still remembers the "wolf lady" and her tame wolves.

*January 10–March 26 Edmonton; visit friends and family in Peace River area; visit Dr. Kenyon at Fort Nelson*

Freer flew to Edmonton on February 4. The doctor drained his ear again and the nurses started the drops. Two days later, Freer started to feel better. On February 17, Freer was discharged from the hospital.

*March 26–May 24 Kechika River valley*

> *Apr 16* The game warden for the Cassiar district "went out to see Ed Johnson about the tame wolves. Game warden landed at Johnson's and then went south."
>
> *Apr 19* "Eddie and Judy were over for my birthday. Judy made a cake. We just had a plain supper and had a couple of drinks, had an enjoyable evening."

Freer had employment with the BC Forest Service on their forest inventory again, although this time it would be for the entire field season. He would be doing the same work as the previous summer, but it would be mainly around Babine Lake. Freer spent most of his time in early May getting ready for the summer since he would not return to the Kechika until the fall.

*May 24–October 30 Forest Inventory Project at Babine Lake and surrounding area*

> *May 24* Freer arrived at Babine Lake. "We worked all day getting the camp together. The boat I used last year on the Stikine River was brought in from Smithers late tonight."
>
> *May 25* "I got the boat in the water and was out on the lake twice." Freer also recorded that there were "three girls in camp here this year. One here for helping the cook and two for counting trees."

Babine is the longest natural lake in British Columbia and there were many days that entailed a considerable amount of travel. It was often windy, and the lake was rough, particularly in the afternoon.

> *June 2* "I took 3 crews up the north arm of Babine Lake, placed out two crews and took the other over to the mine area, went down past mine, lake very rough by the mine, went to the end of north arm." Freer also "saw several shacks

and one lodge in process of being built for summer fishermen, went up a small river at end of north arm."

*June 9* "The girls came in late and I brought them over for supper. Lots of small Indian boats on the lake." Freer's supervisor was Pete Small again, and his wife was also at the lake. The inventory proceeded smoothly throughout July.

On August 1, Freer met Pete Small at Hetherington's cabin with the boat. They went to the fish weir and saw salmon.

*Aug 24* "All the Indians have big smoke houses going. They are catching lots now."

Most of the forest inventory personnel were students who returned to their classes at the end of August. Some people, including Freer, continued to work through the first part of the fall. The work was the same as during the summer but on a smaller scale.

At the end of the season, Freer started to do the cooking for the remaining people.

*Oct 1* "I am doing the cooking and no casualties so far." Three weeks later, he noted that he had been on the inventory crew for five months.

*Oct 23* "It was a beautiful day today, not a cloud in the sky all day and very warm, no wind. I took a grand tour down to Granisle, Red Bluff, Topley Landing and Hawthorne Bay and returned home, not a ripple on the water and quite warm too. Sure lots of hunters all along the lake."

*Oct 24* "Doing the cooking here for 12 men."

Freer finished the field season on October 27 and arrived at Fireside on October 30.

*Oct 30* Freer learned that "Kenny Porter died this summer in Edmonton and old Jimmy Porter died at the boat landing in his sleep."

## October 30–December 31 Fireside

Freer stayed at Fireside during November.

*Nov 10* Freer noted that he had "made lots of friends this year." Later in the month, he mentioned receiving a letter from Naomi Kenney, one of the three women who had been on the forest inventory crew.

Freer took care of the gas pumps, his usual work at Fireside. The month was uneventful except for one incident.

> *Nov 25* "Louis Boya was knifed and killed by his own daughter, the youngest one."

In early December, Freer went to Fort Nelson where he learned from Dr. Kenyon that his ear was all right.

Freer wrote on December 20 that they had a Christmas lunch for the schoolchildren at the lodge.

> *Dec 21* "There was a turkey supper and dance at the recreation hall and some of them were sure drunk."

> *Dec 25* On Christmas, it was a quiet afternoon, with fourteen people at the table for a meal. "I received playing cards and a shirt from Santa."

# 1975

### *January 1–February 24 Fireside*

At the end of January, Freer received a phone call from Pete Small confirming that he had a seasonal job with the BC Forest Service inventory. Most of his work would be as a cook.

> *Feb 10* Freer received several personal letters "from all over BC and Alberta." This included some of the friendships he made during forest inventory work. Freer also noted that two new payphones had been installed at Fireside.

> *Feb 24* "I turned the Fireside gas pump keys over to young Jerry as I am heading for home."

### *February 24–May 16 Kechika River valley*

Freer spent the morning of February 26 around his cabin.

> *Feb 26* "Judy and Ed went up Horn Lake trail and shot a moose on small lake up there. They sure have to hunt or feed those 3 dogs grub, which costs money. Too expensive. My radio is sure working very good."

> *Mar 29* "Judy and Ed's dogs were over here twice. They were chasing my horses here.... Judy was over baking for the dogs." Freer commented several times in his diary that he could hear the light plant at Scoop Lake every day.

In mid-April, Bridcut flew in with the mail and two power saws for Freer. He had two letters confirming summer employment beginning on May 20 at Smithers. Naomi Kenney, with whom Freer had corresponded since the forest inventory in the Stikine area, wrote that she was going to work in the Yukon. Freer named one of his horses for her.

## May 16–June 2 Prepare for Forest Inventory Project, Yellen Lake area

*May 19* Freer went to the base camp at Tyhee Lake near Smithers where he found "about 30 tents and several trailers." Freer also observed: "Quite a few men and girls came in on plane for this camp and are around 30 people here."

Much of the project this summer was in the Yellen Lake area, which was located northwest of Smithers on the south side of the Nass River. On May 30, Freer and five men flew to this lake. All of Freer's work that summer was in this locale.

## June 2–October 2 Forest Inventory Project

*June 4* "I am doing the cooking and getting the firewood, and cooking on open camp fire."

Float planes flew supplies from Smithers. Helicopters were used to move the crews to most of their stations, as well as Freer's camps. Since there was not much travelling during the second half of the summer, Freer was not as busy. The inventory proceeded smoothly during the summer.

*Aug 27* "Lots of salmon in the river." Freer also noted that he was feeding sixteen people.

Two days later, several people finished their fieldwork for the season. Work continued on a reduced scale during September.

*Sept 3* "Plenty of salmon here now."

*Sept 12* "Not too many salmon left and what are left are badly beaten up and some are dying."

*Sept 13* The next day Freer came out to the base camp at Tyhee Lake. "Had 108 days out in fly camp—no bread—a good summer but wet."

## October 2–December 31 Fireside

On October 2, Freer returned to the Kechika.

*Oct 2* "Apparently Ed Johnson and Judy Drake left a month ago to go to Vancouver as she is to have a baby soon."

On October 4, Freer worked a night shift on the gas pumps. Margo and Ken were short-staffed that fall, so Freer had many days with sixteen-hour shifts. With Willard at the lodge, Ken and Margo decided to take their winter holiday before Christmas, departing on November 27.

*Dec 25* "The Reinhold family had Christmas dinner, also the Hazel and Nick LeBerges.... Everybody worked some here today." The lodge was not very busy between Christmas and New Year's Day. On the last day of 1975, Ken and Margo returned.

Willard Freer on the 1934 Bedaux Expedition. Charles Bedaux hired well-known film maker, Floyd Crosby, for the expedition. Crosby also took photographs, including a portrait photograph of each of the members. This is Freer's picture. Freer was known for almost always wearing a big hat while working. He claimed that it helped keep some of the rain off his shoulders making it easier to work in inclement weather. PA-171477, Library and Archives Canada

# AFTERWORD

The Freer family box of diaries ends in 1972. Willard's diaries for the next three years are located at the Fort Nelson Museum. Freer's obituary indicates that he maintained a diary almost until his death, but the whereabouts of the diaries he kept after 1975 are unknown.

Recently, a seventeen-minute 1977 home movie has been digitized and posted on the Internet. It shows Willard taking a riverboat up the Kechika and Turnagain Rivers. The footage shows the power of the current on sections of these rivers and the size and weight of the riverboats. It gives viewers a sense of riverboat travel, and one can understand why Willard was repairing his wooden boats so often.

Another important event in 1977 was the death of Margo, who was killed in an automobile accident while returning from Fort Nelson in mid-November of that year. Willard wrote a letter to the Nelms describing the incident. In it he said: "She sure will be missed and she worked so hard. Dale came up the day she died to be here and Margo and Ken were going on a holiday November 25 for about 6 weeks to Australia and New Zealand."

Margo was the driving force behind the Fireside Inn, and after her death, Ken had no desire to continue living there. Within a few years, he sold the lodge and moved out of the area. The August 2, 1982, *Whitehorse Daily Star* newspaper reported, "Fire swept over the tiny roadside hamlet of Fireside, destroying a lodge, gas station and several residences. About 30 people were evacuated Friday from the community.... The fire burned telephone lines and cut communications to the village."

After Ken left Fireside, Willard moved to the nearby Coal River Lodge at Mile 533, where he worked up until the last few weeks of his life pumping gas and cooking.

Willard died in 1981. His obituary in the *Fort Nelson News* follows the pioneer theme with the headline "A Trailblazer Passes." The article stated: "During his life, Willard kept a full diary and journal of the daily happenings, including weather and precipitation, which is a permanent record of his unusual life in the wilderness." It noted that he was "proficient in wilderness travel" and stated that "he trapped, guided, freighted and traded. He was an excellent horseman and riverman."

Eighty years ago, Willard Freer first came to the Kechika River valley. The Indigenous inhabitants were still largely following their seasonal activities, and he recorded his encounters with them. Some of the people, like Louis Boya and Amos Alec, have over a hundred notations in Freer's diaries through more than twenty-five years. Despite living in a wilderness area, the Alaska Highway and the bush airplane dramatically changed the way of life of the Indigenous inhabitants, and Freer noted this. Freer spent time along the Alaska Highway in the late 1950s, 1960s and 1970s, particularly at the Fireside Inn. Those were peak years of tourist travel along this highway when there were many lodges along the route, and Freer described the daily activities at the lodge where he was working.

Freer's unique written record, along with Skook Davidson's newly located material and the riverboat film footage, will be accessible on the Internet and will provide readers with a considerable amount of previously unpublished material to explore. It is a fortuitous time for people who are interested in the history of the area.

Darwin Cary, who owns Scoop Lake Outfitters, writes that there is a hill on the east side of the Kechika River that is still called Willard's Hill. Cary also states that "some of Willard's horses still live in the area, a few generations removed." Willard would be pleased to know that descendants of his horses still live in the valley and that he still has a presence there.

# Official BC Geographical Names

The places below were named for individuals mentioned in Freer's diaries. The quotations below were obtained from the BC Geographical Names website, https://apps.gov.bc.ca/pub/bcgnws/web/.

**Boya**
Boya Creek
"Named after Louis Boya, whose hunting territory or trap lines were here."

**Bronlund**
Bronlund Creek, Bronlund Peak
"Bronlund Peak named in 1931 by F.C. Swannell, BCLS, after Emil Bronlund, mining engineer for the Consolidated Mining and Smelting Company of Trail, who was presumably working in the Cassiar area at the time."

**Davidson (Skook)**
Mount Skook Davidson
"Named for John Ogilvie ('Skookum') Davidson (1892–1972).... This mountain overlooks Skook's Diamond J Ranch, across the Kechika River just below Terminus Mountain."

**Skooks Landing**
"Skook Davidson established this landing after the Alaska Highway was completed in 1943.... Skook would arrange for supplies to be set down on the highway there, pack them down a short trail to the landing, and boat them 150 miles up the Kechika River to his Diamond J Ranch. He used the landing until 1972."

**Forsberg**
Forsberg Ridge, Forsberg Creek
"Named in 1940 by N.C. Stewart, BCLS, after Fred Forsberg, a trapper."

**Freer**
Freer Creek (BC and Yukon)
"Named after Willard Freer, who packed in this area during the 1947 BC-Yukon boundary survey."

**Ludwig**
Ludwig Creek
Named "… after Ludwig Smaaslet, a trapper."

**McCook**
McCook River, Mount McCook
"Named after the McCook family who trapped in the Kechika–Gataga River areas and lived at Fort Ware."

# INDIGENOUS NAMES RECORDED IN FREER'S DIARIES

This list identifies the Indigenous inhabitants that Freer named in his diary entries. Any errors are the responsibility of the author.

A more detailed individual list will be posted on the Northern BC Archives website. It will include the dates of every entry Freer has in his diaries with that Indigenous person, in chronological order.

Abou, Charles
Abou, Daisy
Abou, Ernest
Abou, Frank
Abou, George
Abou, Gordon
Abou, Jack
Abou, Mrs. Jack (Louise?)
Abou, Margaret
Abou, Roy
Abou children
Alec(k), Amos
Alec, Chief
Alec, Dempsey
Alec, Elsie
Alec, Emma
Alec, Maggie
Alec, Margaret
Allen, Ann
Allen, Bill
Allen, Tom
Bob, Andrew
Boya, Charlie
Boya, Joe
Boya, Louis
Boya family
Boya, Margaret
Boya, Minnie
Boya, Mrs. Louis
Boya, Rose

Boya, Vera
Carlick, Fred (Loudecker?)
Charlie, Alan/Allen
Charlie, Francis
Charlie, Henry
Dennis, Thomas
Edzerza, Chris
Edzerza, Don
Edzerza, George
Edzerza, Gerald
Edzerza, June
Edzerza, Liz
Forsberg, Annie and Fred
Frank, Amy
Frank, Anne
Frank, Arnold
Frank, Benny
Frank, Ernie
Frank, Hilda
Frank, Mabel
Frank, Perry
Frank, Tommy
Gauthier, Yvonne
George, Dan
George, Don
George, Ella
George, Frank
George, Jack
George, Stan
George boy

Groat, Buster
Hayes, Emma
Hayes, Joe
John, Henry
Johnnie, David
Johnnie, Edward
Johnnie, Felix
Johnnie, Harry
Johnnie, John
Johnnie, Leo
Johnnie, Mike
Johnnie, Vincent
Johnnie outfit
Loudecker, Fred (Carlick?)
Lutz, Barney
Lutz, Daisy
MacDonald
MacDonald, Alec?
MacDonald, Pete
Massetoe, Amos
Massetoe, George
Massetoe, Jimmy?
Massetoe, Jim
Massetoe, Perry
Massetoe boy
McCook, Alan
McCook, Craig
McCook, Donald
McCook, Elmer
McCook, Emil
McCook, Fred
McCook, Jim
McCook, Joe
McCook, John
McCook, Melvin
McCook, Michel
McCook family
McCook, Old (Mac)
McWilliam, Fred
Merchant, Annie
Merchant, Guy
Miller, Don
Miller, Eddie
Miller, Leo?
Pete, Ann

Pete, Charlie (daughter Louis Boya?)
Pie, Douglas
Pie, Johnnie
Poole, John
Poole, Pat
Porter boys
Porter, Betsy
Porter, Bob
Porter, Brian
Porter, Charlie
Porter, Charlie (young)
Porter, Dempsey
Porter, Dennis
Porter children
Porter, Ella
Porter, George
Porter, Harry/Henry
Porter, Jimmie
Porter, John
Porter, Ken
Porter, Lucy
Porter, Minnie
Porter, Murphy
Porter (old lady)
Reid, Douglas
Stone, Andy
Stone, Frank
Stone, Maggie
Williams, Dick?
Williams, Jock?
Williams, Mike

# Sources Consulted

## Archives and Museums

Item CM/S2, Trapline sketches of Central and Northern British Columbia, 1922–1972, BC Archives.

Willard Freer Diary, 1973–1975, Fort Nelson Heritage Museum.

Field Notebooks, Hu Gabrielse, Geological Survey of Canada, Vancouver office.

C.H. Ney Field Diary, 1944, Land Title and Survey Authority (British Columbia).

John Leslie Charles fonds, box 1, folder 8, correspondence; box 2, folder 7, *Report on the Preliminary Reconnaissance of Feasible Railway Route— Northern BC*, University of Manitoba.

## BC Sessional Papers

Campbell, A.J. "British Columbia-Yukon Boundary Survey." Department of Lands and Forests, 1947, pp. X109–117.

Campbell, A.J. "British Columbia-Yukon Boundary Survey." Report of the Deputy Minister of Lands, 1948, pp. X136–143.

Campbell, A.J. "British Columbia-Yukon Boundary Survey." Report of the Deputy Minister of Lands, 1949, pp. U151–158.

Pattinson, Hugh. "Triangulation Control Survey, Covering Part of Drainage Area of Upper Skeena and Nass Rivers, Cassiar District." Report of Minister of Lands, 1943, pp. C34–37.

Province of British Columbia. *Provincial Game Commission Report 1950*, p. 29.

"Rex vs. Poole, Stephen (murder)." Reports of the Commissioner of Provincial Police for the Year 1943 and Inspector of Gaols. Victoria: King's Printer, 1945, pp. W15–16.

Swannell, Frank. "Triangulation Survey, Cassiar District." Report of Minister of Lands, 1939, pp. V30–33.

## Books

Barr, David. *One Lucky Canuck: An Autobiography*. Victoria: Trafford Publishing, 2004.

Billington, Keith. *Tse-Loh-Ne: The People at the End of the Rocks*. Halfmoon Bay, BC: Caitlin Press, 2012.

Cooke, Frank. *Wild & Free: Frank Cooke, as Told to Jack Boudreau.* Prince George, BC: Caitlin Press, 2002.

Cummins, Bryan. *Faces of the North: The Ethnic Photography of John Honigmann.* Toronto: Natural Heritage/Natural History, 2004.

Farrow, Moira. *Nobody Here but Us: Pioneers of the North.* Vancouver: J.J. Douglas, 1975.

Fiennes, Ranulph. *The Headless Valley.* London: Hodder and Stoughton, 1973.

Gontard, Lily. *Beyond Mile Zero: The Vanishing Alaska Highway Lodge Community.* Madeira Park, BC: Lost Moose Publishing, 2017.

Patterson, R.M. *Finlay's River.* New York: William Morrow, 1968.

Reierson, Clem. *From Vanderhoof to Lower Post.* Victoria: Friesen Press, 2014.

*Report of the Commission Appointed to Delimit the Boundary between the Province of British Columbia and the Yukon and Northwest Territories.* Ottawa: Queen's Printer, 1966.

Rutledge, Leo. *That Some May Follow: The History of Guide Outfitting in British Columbia,* 2nd ed. Richmond, BC: Guide Outfitters Association of British Columbia, ca. 2004.

Sawchuk, Wayne. *Crossing the Divide: Discovering a Wilderness Ethic in Canada's Northern Rockies.* Smithers, BC: Creekstone Press, 2020.

Ventress, Cora, Marguerite Davies, and Edith Kyllo. *The Peacemakers of North Peace* (Hudson's Hope Section). Hudson's Hope, BC: The Authors, 1973.

Ward, Bud. *Bud's Story: Game Warden to CO.* Vancouver: Talus Publishing Group, 2008.

## FAMILY COLLECTIONS

Willard Freer family: diaries, 1942–1973, photographs

Skook Davidson family: diary fragments; photographs; fur trade ledger book, 1945–1948

Clem Reierson family: correspondence with Skook Davidson

Don Peck family: correspondence with Skook Davidson

## BOOKLETS, MAGAZINE ARTICLES, REPORTS AND THESES

*Alaska Highway: Road to Yukon Adventure. 1959.* Ottawa: Canadian Government Travel Bureau.

Barr, D.A. "Axel Showing, NWT." Northwestern Explorations, 1955.

"Jack & Flo Christy: Pioneers of the Alaska Highway." *The Yukoner Magazine,* no. 23, August 2002.

Nelms, Joyce. "The Indian Woman and Household Structure in Mill Creek, British Columbia." MA thesis, University of Victoria, 1977, 84 leaves.

Swannell, Arthur. "Skookum Davidson." *The Link*, vol. 1, no. 3, December 1977, pp. 36–40.

Weaver, John. *The Greater Muskwa-Kechika: Building a Better Network for Protecting Wildlife and Wilderness.* Wildlife Conservation Society Canada Conservation Report #13, July 2019.

Weaver, John. "Muskwa-Kechika: An Opportunity for Bold Conservation Action." *Canadian Geographic*, September 24, 2019, https://canadian.geographic.ca/articles/muskwa-kechika-an-opportunity-for-bold-conservation-action/.

## NEWSPAPER ARTICLES (CHRONOLOGICAL ORDER)

July 9, 1942, *Prince George Citizen*, "Will Complete Railway Survey by October 1," p.1.

October 7, 1943, *Prince George Citizen*, "Poole Guilty Manslaughter; Sentenced to Life in Prison: Jury finds Fort Ware Native guilty of slaying wife on January 8 last—Tragedy follows drinking party at lonely northern outpost—accused denies knowledge of crime," p.1.

December 14, 1959, *Prince George Citizen*, "Santa Flies 610 Miles to Northern Christmas Party," p. 1.

December 19, 1962, *Prince George Citizen*, "Children again dub 'Reindeer' Smashing Success," p. 1.

July 11, 1963, *Whitehorse Daily Star*, "Alaska Highway Washouts Close Route To All Traffic," p. 1.

January 19, 1965, *Vancouver Sun*, "Two Children Die on Trail," p. 1.

January 19, 1965, *Brandon (Manitoba) Sun*, "Tragic Story Unfolds," p. 1.

January 20, 1965, *Victoria Daily Colonist*, "Heroic Trek in Vain: Sick Children Die on Trail," p. 3.

May 2, 1966, *Tallahassee Democrat*, "Search Continues for Missing Pilot," p. 4.

August 6, 1969, *Sioux City (Iowa) Journal*, "Horseman on Trip of 4400 Miles," p. 19.

December 19, 1969, *St. Joseph (Missouri) News-Press*, "Horse Used in Journey Missing," p. 2.

December 3, 1974, *Prince George Citizen*, "Lower Post Rejects Operation Reindeer," p. 3.

January 12, 1976, *Whitehorse Daily Star*, "No Inquest Planned into Freezing Deaths," p. 16.

September 30, 1981, *Fort Nelson News*, "A Trail Blazer Passes," p. 14.

August 2, 1982, *Whitehorse Daily Star*, "Fire Burning Out of Control," p. 1.

# INDEX

# ACKNOWLEDGEMENTS

For a book that mentions a variety of individuals over a period of more than thirty years, there are many people who I would like to thank for their invaluable assistance. Beth Summers, Willard Freer's niece, loaned me his diaries and gave me permission to use them for the book. Without Beth's assistance, this book would not have been written. I would also like to thank other members of Freer's family who provided assistance in locating some of Freer's photographs.

Dr. Daniel Sims, associate professor in the First Nations program at the University of Northern British Columbia (UNBC) and a member of the Tsay Keh Dene First Nation, read most of the sections related to the Indigenous inhabitants of the area around the Finlay and Kechika Rivers and provided comments and corrections. Dr. Sims's input was very beneficial; I appreciated his willingness to share his knowledge and expertise, particularly regarding the intricacies of Indigenous names. Any errors are my responsibility. Thank you. Mike Gillingham, UNBC, produced the excellent maps at the beginning of the book.

My thanks also go to Ross Peck, chairman of the Muskwa-Kechika Advisory Board from 2001 to 2007 and former president of the Hudson's Hope Historical Society. He knew about the existence of Willard Freer's diaries and put me in contact with Beth Summers, Willard's niece. Ross has extensive knowledge of the history of northern BC and once again gave me sources of information that I did not know about. I also appreciate Ross's input and comments on portions of this manuscript. Ross has been involved with several books that I have produced, and I always enjoy working with him.

In the 1960s and 1970s, Freer spent part of almost every year at the Fireside Inn. Dale Windrem, son of Ken and Margo Windrem (Ken and Margo owned the Fireside Inn for about twenty years), shared his memories of Fireside and loaned me pictures for the book. Joyce Nelms Matzke, daughter of George and Violet Nelms, also shared her memories and loaned me visual material. (George was the highway maintenance supervisor in the Fireside community for many years.) My thanks to both of you for your information and recollections about Fireside.

In the spring of 2021, I received a phone call from Gord Yule. His great-uncle was Skook Davidson, and he had a box of Skook's material that had survived the fire that destroyed his ranch. Gord lent me the box for a few months. It contained photos, diary fragments and other material, and provided new perspectives on Skook that I have incorporated into the book. This material now resides in the Northern BC Archives in Prince George and will eventually be put online for the public to access. My thanks to Gord for sharing this valuable Skook Davidson information.

Willard Freer packed for Hu Gabrielse of the Canadian Geological Survey for four summers. Hu did an interview with me and loaned me his photographs of the years from 1958 to 1961, when Freer was on his crew. The Geological Survey library in Vancouver has material that provides details regarding Gabrielse's work during these four years, and Hu and I spent time at the library one afternoon looking at this information. My thanks go to Hu; Warren Wulff, Library Manager, Natural Resources Canada, Vancouver; and the library staff for their assistance.

I would like to express my appreciation to Darwin Cary of Scoop Lake Outfitters for sharing his extensive knowledge and memories of the Kechika.

My thanks also go to Sharon Keen, who did several hours of volunteer research. I particularly appreciate the information she located related to the traplines in the Kechika River valley.

I would like to thank Chris Widrig for the information that he provided about several of the Indigenous inhabitants of the Kechika and for the photograph of Amos Alec and his family.

In 2018 my wife and I spent an afternoon with Clem Reierson and his wife, Ruby, at Enderby, BC. Clem shared his memories of being at the Diamond J Ranch in the late fall and winter of 1954–55, which I greatly appreciate.

I would like to express my appreciation to everyone else who assisted.

Finally, I would like to thank Vici Johnstone and Caitlin Press for publishing this book, and to my patient wife, Linda, for the myriad of ways in which she has again assisted me.

# ABOUT THE AUTHOR

Jay Sherwood (1947-2022) started his career in surveying before becoming a teacher-librarian. In his retirement, he authored twelve books on BC history, including the four-book series about the career of surveyor Frank Swannell. Two of his works have been BC Book Prize finalists, and three have received BC Historical Federation awards. *Ootsa Lake Odyssey* (Caitlin Press, 2016) won the 2018 Jeanne Clarke Memorial local history award. His most recent publications include the two-part series on the Alberta/BC boundary survey, and his final publication is *Kechika Chronicler: Willard Freer's Northern BC and Yukon Diaries, 1942-1975.*